Crawl Before You Ball ™

Breaking the Cycle of Generational Poverty

BUFFIE PURSELLE

Crawl Before You Ball: Breaking the Cycle of Generational Poverty
© 2022, Buffie Purselle. All rights reserved.

Published by MrsMD, Atlanta, Georgia

979-8-9857598-0-8 (paperback)
979-8-9857598-1-5 (eBook)
Library of Congress Control Number: 2022903635

For more information, email hola@buffiellc.com.

CONTENTS

Foreword.. i

Introduction...1

CHAPTER 1 The Importance of Addressing Your
Financial Mental Health 9

CHAPTER 2 What Had Happened Was.............................31

CHAPTER 3 Codependent Poverty 39

CHAPTER 4 Check Yo'self with Empathy! 57

CHAPTER 5 The Crawling Phase—Needs vs. Wants........77

CHAPTER 6 The Most Important Investment You
Will Ever Make 93

CHAPTER 7 The Investment of Generational Wealth 105

CHAPTER 8 Discover Your New Normal.........................115

30-Day Financial Detox Journal 123

Acknowledgments..185

Meet Buffie...187

FOREWORD

AS A PSYCHIATRIST AND MENTAL HEALTH EXPERT,
I have spent many years talking to people about their struggles with depression and anxiety as well as a variety of other illnesses. Identifying the stressors with which one is dealing is a routine part of any mental health assessment. One of the most common and particularly problematic stressors is financial stress. The constant worry about paying for rent, utilities, and the kids' school supplies often leads to feelings of hopelessness and helplessness. These difficult feelings can impair one to the point of complacency and resignation to a life of financial struggle.

If you are reading this book, this probably sounds all too familiar. You may be thinking, Yeah, that's me, but how do I get out of this? You may say to yourself, "I just need to make more money to make ends meet." While this sounds like a good (but maybe impractical) solution, the chances are that more income will not solve the problem. In this book, Buffie addresses this issue head-on. She has spent years in various financial services and is a nationally recognized financial and tax expert. Don't believe me? Well, all you have to do is look for her appearances on networks such as CNN, HLN, and CNBC. Throughout her career, Buffie has helped thousands of people with their financial needs. This has helped her develop a deep and unique understanding of the real cause for many money woes—a dysfunctional relationship with money. Being married to Buffie for many years has given me the privilege of intimately witnessing the development and evolution of the *Crawl Before You Ball* program that helps you understand why you have money problems and what you can do about it.

Now, if all you want is a budgeting book, a guide to tell you how to add your income, subtract your expenses, balance your checkbook, or get your financial app to stop showing minus signs in front of the numbers, this may not be the book for you. But if you want to understand how you got into your financial mess, what keeps you there, and what you can do to make fundamental changes in your relationship with money, then keep reading. As a word of warning, I have seen firsthand that this program can be emotionally challenging, as it forces you to look at yourself and the behaviors that keep you in constant financial turmoil. It can be hard on you and possibly your significant others when you set the boundaries and make the necessary changes to achieve lasting success. But, if you want to make a real change, you have to understand and modify the maladaptive behaviors that keep you in constant money struggles. *Crawl Before You Ball* is the book that will get you there.

David C. Purselle, MD, MSCR

INTRODUCTION

IF YOU ARE SOMEONE WHO experiences relentless, gut-wrenching, paralyzing dread on the first and fifteenth of each month, I wrote this book for you. Whether your angst is derived solely from your own fiscal fuck-ups, or you are afraid to answer your phone, view text messages, or answer your front door for fear that someone you know, or love, will inundate you with their story of biweekly economic disaster, *Crawl Before You Ball* is for you. Most of our brains have been pre-programmed to think life equals survival, not fulfillment, not peace, and certainly not happiness. This deeply saddens me. I believe that anyone, no matter their socioeconomic status, can live a life full of joy and free from the economic stressors that cause us to be miserable for no damn reason.

I believe you *can* have it all as long as *you* and not others craft the definition of the word ALL. If someone is a financial guru, I believe they've worked on their own monetary mental health and not by being a budgeting conformist. Again, life is for living, not only for surviving. *Crawl Before*

You Ball is a way of truly living the life you wish to have. I believe we must crawl BEFORE we ball. There are some things in life that we *have* to do, and once we do them, we can do whatever the hell we desire later. Unfortunately, we are taught that delayed gratification is bad. We have been taught that *instagramification* is the way of the land. Everything we see, hear, smell, and taste reinforces this faux belief system, which is all by design to keep us in a constant state of helplessness.

Why You Should Listen to My Arse

1682 Likes

So, why should you listen to me? My name is Buffie Purselle. Yes, Buffie is my real name. My mother liked an old show from the early seventies called *Family Affair*. One of the daughters on the show was named Buffy, a cute little girl with pigtails, so that's from whence my name came. I have been a fintech expert specializing in tax and personal finance for over twenty years. I am a nationally recognized financial expert who has appeared on CNBC, HLN, and CNN.

My passion for finance began while working in my family's tax business at age sixteen. I worked on weekends, after school during tax season, and I helped with tax planning during the summer. I instantly understood the business and was able to connect with clients quickly. My grandmother said it was as if I had been there before in a former life, working in my old position. I loved helping people with their taxes; however, as time went on, I realized a few things I wanted to do differently from my family. So, when I graduated from high school and began college, I opened my very own first branch. It was a tiny hole-in-the-wall office with no windows in a small town in South Atlanta. I loved it! It was all mine, and I easily managed the $900 per month office rent.

My family was shocked when I left the security of the family business to do my own thing, but I knew it was what I had to do. I learned Spanish and became the first IRS Acceptance Agent in town. The IRS licenses Acceptance Agents to issue tax ID numbers, and tax ID numbers enable undocumented people to file their taxes legally. There was a considerable demand for this service in South Atlanta. I began with zero clients and quickly grew the practice to over five thousand. Soon after, at age twenty, I became a licensed mortgage broker. Qualifying to become a licensed mortgage broker required passing a series of challenging exams, having excellent credit, and maintaining a high net worth. It was a complicated process, especially at my age. I then had to hire and train enough employees to navigate the very rigid guidelines of loan origination.

Business was booming, so I opened another office in another small town in South Atlanta and hired staff. I had loan officers, loan processors, assistants, and interpreters working beside me each day, helping our clients achieve the goal of homeownership. And because of my tax and accounting background, we knew how to provide meaningful services for our clients. We didn't allow our clients to get into horrible mortgages that we knew they could not afford. I even became a licensed life, health, property, and casualty agent.

I was quickly heading a full-service, highly successful financial business. This made me happy because not only was I helping folks become more financially independent, but I was also providing jobs for people in my community who looked like me—just as my grandmother had done.

I bought my first home when I was nineteen. It had three bedrooms, which I quickly realized I didn't need, so I rented out one bedroom to my cousin. Having my cousin as a housemate enabled me to split the low mortgage of $600 per month. My cousin also helped pay for utilities. I liked seeing my home appreciate while paying a fraction of what it would cost someone to rent an apartment. In fact, I liked it so much that I started purchasing other properties—another lesson I learned from my grandmother.

Fast forward to my more recent endeavors: I have appeared on two reality TV shows. One was a business competition with a billionaire looking for a business partner. It was similar to *The Apprentice*. I did incredibly well and made it to the top four before leaving the show. I also decided to make an appearance as a friend on Bravo's *Married to Medicine,* which I will refer to as *That Show* from here on out. That little stint was very traumatic for me, so please be advised that I will likely shade those broads a few times in this book; it's called closure. I'll get more into my past shortly because for **Crawl Before You Ball** to work, we must be totally honest with each other. Most importantly, we must be honest with ourselves.

Speaking of honesty, I am *real*. Some might say *too* real. And what I have to say about personal finance is *really* real. My writing style is exactly how I speak. I curse and use slang and colloquialisms quite a bit. There will be a number of long sentences (much to the chagrin of my book editor) that I felt needed to be included for emphasis. In the pages ahead, I won't conform to societal norms of how a book should look or be. In this book, I share excerpts of student homework from my digital course. I also use "so" more often than I probably should, SO get used to it. Also note, I wrote an earlier draft of this book over a decade ago and have included excerpts from that version. If you read something that seems old—for example, if I mention Blockbuster Video or say something about my nephews who are now grown men—that's why. When you come across these passages, I would like you to think of the modern equivalent of whatever I am writing. I didn't change a single word of these excerpts because "I'm an artist, and I'm sensitive about my shit." —Erykah Badu.

> **The Breakdown: WTH Is** *Crawl Before You Ball?*

♡ ◯ ◁   ◻

Likes 5698

Now that you know a little more about why you made the right decision to listen to my arse, let me tell you what the hell is *Crawl Before You Ball* (CB4UB). (I know the U should be a Y, but again, I'm weird.) Do you remember when you were young and got in trouble for not doing your homework and chores? I do. I vividly remember my mother telling my younger sister and me that we had to do our chores and homework before we could have fun and play outside. Her saying that over and over again stuck with me. She was basically saying the following: do what you *have* to do so you can do what you *want* to do later, a.k.a. ***Crawl Before You Ball***. Most people think CB4UB is only about money and "balling out" with your finances—disregarding your budget and allowing your emotions and whims to rule your finances. It's not. It's a new way of life. In the next however many pages I decide to type, I hope that I can help you change your relationship with money for good.

It Was Never About a Budget

Likes 4095

When the average personal financial adviser begins working with their clients, they usually start with the almighty budget. You know, that responsible thing that we are all *supposed* to do each month? I could not disagree more. I believe that everyone with at least a sixth-grade education understands that if Suzy wants an apple that costs a dollar and she only has fifty cents, Suzy cannot afford the apple, right? The real problem lies in why Suzy wants the apple and why she will likely beg, borrow, and in some cases steal to get the other fifty cents to purchase that shiny, delicious red apple. This problem is why some of you may have read all those other books, attended countless expensive seminars, and are still in the same financial predicament you were in when you began your journey.

To fix this problem, we must get into the *why* before getting into the *how*. It is extremely important that before you embark on this financial journey with me, you understand that it will be unlike anything you have ever done before. I will not dedicate your most valuable asset—your time— to things you already know. We have to work *first* on the uncomfortable stuff that causes you to continue fucking up each month. Remember, I told you I have a potty mouth. I get real. And I personally don't trust people who don't feel free enough to use all of the English language when writing or speaking. So, if this offends you, you should probably stop reading now.

> **Insane in the Brain**

Likes 34234

All righty, now that you know who I am, what I have done, and my philosophy on financial literacy, let's talk about the real topic of this book: our brains. The definition of insanity is doing the same thing over and over again and expecting a different result. I don't think people realize this. How can they? Why would they continue to practice insanity with their finances year after year if they did?

"If I could just win the lottery, everything would be OK."
"I just need one big break."
"It seems like everyone else is living the good life, and I'm always struggling to make it from week to week. It's not fair!"

I can't tell you how often I have heard clients, family members, and friends say these things to me. And I have to admit, there was also a time in my life when I said those things to myself. It took me years of insanity to finally realize that the solution to my problem was all in my head.

So, as you read through this book and begin your CB4UB journey, I recommend seeing a mental health specialist for help with any significant financial anxiety, stress, depression, or trauma. Doing so has certainly helped me.

CHAPTER 1

THE IMPORTANCE OF ADDRESSING YOUR FINANCIAL MENTAL HEALTH

LET'S GET INTO IT! First, I want to discuss your financial mental health. Yep, you read that correctly. Let's talk about your financial mental health because no one else does, and, frankly, it is the underlying reason you have a screwed-up relationship with money.

I have never understood why mental health is considered a taboo topic. Having anxiety or suffering from depression is not a freaking weakness. I am so sick of that assertion because your brain controls everything in your body, right? If the thing that controls your entire body isn't functioning properly, then, of course, everything else in your life will be jacked up. It's so simple that it is actually a tad scary. Of course, I may be a little bit biased given that I live with a brilliant psychiatrist, but a bih knows what she's talking about!

I have a suspicion that society or SocieTHEY, as I call it, doesn't want you to understand the importance of mental health because when you finally do, you will be able to do anything in this world that you want. We stop ourselves from achieving our goals 99 percent of the time because of anxiety, depression, and post-traumatic stress disorder (PTSD). We must take care of our brains.

Speaking of PTSD, the love of my life, and occasional bane of my existence, the renowned psychiatrist David Purselle, MD, MSCR, has said to me repeatedly that he does not believe financial PTSD meets the clinical definition of PTSD. Now, I am just a mere MrsMD, but if the powers that be took the time to do a study or two (wink, wink, Dr. Purselle), they would see that being chronically stressed the hell out about money qualifies as PTSD.

The American Psychiatric Association defines PTSD as "a psychiatric disorder that may occur in people who have experienced or witnessed a traumatic event, such as a natural disaster, a severe accident, a terrorist act, war/combat, or rape, or who have been threatened with death, sexual violence, or serious injury."

According to psychiatry.org, PTSD has been known by many names in the past, such as "shell shock" during the years of World War I and "combat fatigue" after World War II, but PTSD does not just happen to combat veterans. PTSD can occur in all people of any ethnicity, nationality, culture, and age. PTSD affects approximately 3.5 percent of U.S. adults every year, and an estimated one in eleven people will be diagnosed with PTSD in their lifetime.

Crawl Before You Ball

People with PTSD have intense, disturbing thoughts and feelings related to their experience that last long after the traumatic event. They may relive the event through flashbacks or nightmares; they may feel sadness, fear, or anger. They may even feel detached or estranged from other people. People with PTSD may avoid situations or people that remind them of the traumatic event, and they may have strong adverse reactions to something as ordinary as a loud noise or an accidental touch.

A diagnosis of PTSD requires exposure to an upsetting, traumatic event. However, the exposure could be indirect rather than firsthand. For example, PTSD can occur in individuals learning about the violent death of a close family member or friend. It can also happen because of repeated exposure to horrible details of a trauma, such as police officers who are exposed to the details of child abuse cases.

Now, I am well aware that folks will think me a bit theatrical with my MrsMD diagnosis of financial PTSD, but let's have some discourse on the subject. Trust me, there have been hours and hours of calm discussions in our home that turned into histrionic arguments over this very topic. I am well aware that I do not have an MD, but I am a Capricorn and will prove my damn case.

If you grew up seeing your parents live paycheck to paycheck and have a horrible relationship with money, chances are you will too. I teach CB4UB as a digital course, and a student recently introduced me to a term she used while growing up—"money sickness." Money sickness was a term she came up with as a kid after witnessing her mother's inability to function due to crippling financial stress. Her mother was so "sick" that she and her sister had to care for themselves and their mother. She said her mother would cry and couldn't get out of bed. This happened throughout her childhood, around the first and fifteenth of each month. Some might say money sickness is merely anxiety and depression. I believe that chronic stress over money can lead to trauma-like symptoms. The fact that you are so stressed out about money that you take to the bed each month, and your kids have diagnosed you with money sickness, tells me there is trauma. If that's not trauma, I don't know what is. My student also indicated that now as an adult, like her mother, she also experiences a range of debilitating emotions, including nightmares and fatigue, around the first and fifteenth of each month. This occurs even though she is financially stable and has no issues with paying her bills. I firmly believe the repeated exposure as a child of watching her mother struggle with "money sickness" still affects her to this day.

Throughout my career, I have seen clients with financial mental health issues ranging from depression to severe anxiety; in fact, one client was rushed to the emergency room via ambulance because he thought he was having a heart attack. And since you bought my book, I gather that you are currently experiencing some level of financial stress or trauma—or perhaps someone close to you is. Maybe it doesn't meet the *exact* definition of PTSD, but no one can deny that connections exist between money, trauma, and severe stress, so for now, let's pretend I am correct.

When you work your ass off to care for yourself and your family and have a stack of bills you can't pay, you can't help but feel a sense of hopelessness, a sense of worthlessness. Why do I keep failing when everyone around me *seems* like they have it all figured out? Well, let me tell you: most people *don't* have it figured out. Most people are in the same situation as you. My students have indicated that by doing our weekly live calls, they realized that regardless of their socioeconomic backgrounds, they all had in common a poor relationship with money. So if you're suffering from ongoing financial stress, I hope this provides you with a sense of community. And let's be real: community is necessary when tackling any mental health condition, which is one reason group therapy can be so effective.

Perception Is Rarely Reality

♡ ◯ ◁   ⊓

Likes 9696

I remember being at a gas station and meeting someone who saw me on *That Show*.

"This is your car, Buffie?" The young lady was giving my sweet Bessie a serious side-eye.

Now, if you follow me on social media, you know about my beloved car daughter, Bessie; may she rest in auto heaven. Before my husband, David, murdered her, I was happily driving her in the city as if she were new.

"Yes, this is my car," I said, beaming with pride. I truly loved Bessie. Yes, Bessie was a fifteen-year-old car baby. She had ripped pleather seats and broken air conditioning vents that I refused to fix, but to me, she looked and smelled like the day that David first started driving her.

"But I thought that you were rich?"

I laughed so hard. "Oh, honey, I don't have enough time today to tell you how what you just said is so darn silly, but thanks for saying hi." Bessie and I drove off, chuckling as we headed home to our mansion.

See, I was totally unbothered by her ignorance and almost felt sorry for her because I come from a community of people who view appreciating assets like real estate as something for which you should be proud, but not a car.

Bessie was an adopted car daughter that I didn't have to pay one single cent to love. When David wanted a new car, we got him a Tesla, and I adopted Bessie. Nobody could tell me she wasn't beautiful. After having open engine surgery twice, my mechanic told me that he would not do any more engine transplants on her and that I needed to lay her to rest. I think he and David came up with this plan to kill her, but alas, my point is—reality is what *you* think and feel.

When you feel the spirit of envy and hate your car or the home you live in, channel the *feeling* that you had when you longed to live or drive what you currently have. The problem with some humans is that we crave stuff, and when we finally get it, we become quickly unsatisfied. The "new car smell," for lack of a better phrase, dissipates. It's kind of like Shiny Ball Syndrome. We're always longing for something else, something better. But who says it's better? SocieTHEY! SocieTHEY tells you this with deceptive marketing tricks and social media tactics (which we will discuss in-depth later). Don't allow it.

We must block out the societal pressure to show folks what we have. While driving Bessie virtually for free (except for her medical bills), I was able to invest my money in real estate that, to this day, makes me money while I sleep. Of course, no one can *see* that when I'm driving around town, but *I know*—and that's all that matters. Be in the spirit of gratitude for what you *do* have. So, walk around your home or apartment and envision it as the place you think you want. You might just manifest it in your life.

Forgive Yo'self, Child

Likes 6963

Why do we treat ourselves so poorly? I am definitely guilty of this horrible human flaw. I will give other people the benefit of the doubt over and over again, but when I fiscally mess up, baaaaaby, you would think I killed someone with the amount of guilt and disappointment I have in myself. During our weekly CB4UB Zooms, I noticed that whenever a student decides to be brave enough to share their experience with the group, they always blame themselves for bad prior financial behavior, almost horrifically so. I have interrupted many a student whilst they were mid-sentence because I was struck by how ruthlessly hard they were on themselves when sharing their #whathadhappenedwas. You will learn about #whathadhappenedwas in more detail in the next chapter, but, basically, it's stating out loud how you got yourself in the financial situation you are currently in. It's kind of like the famous Alcoholics Anonymous introduction. "Hi, I'm so-and-so, and I'm an alcoholic." It's a confession and a statement of acceptance.

Listen, we have all fucked up, me included. But we can't progress if we stay in a place of perpetual blame. I will type that again because I want this statement to resonate with you on a deep level: *We can't progress if we stay in a place of perpetual blame.* You will have financial setbacks in your life, and that's OK. Please take this moment to forgive yourself. I want you to write it below in the space provided, then say it back to yourself whenever you falter. And trust me, you will falter. We all do. We are humans, not damn robots. After writing your forgiveness mantra, I want you to memorize it and say it to yourself whenever financial challenges arise. And because you have trusted me with your journey to financial freedom, I will share with you my forgiveness mantra:

> *I rebuke the guilt and shame that I have attached to the fiscal fuck-ups in my life. I am grateful for those*

*mistakes because they are lessons that I must
learn along the path to living the life I truly desire.*

To this day, I still say it to myself when I am in a financial dilemma.

Now, it's your turn. Please use the space below to forgive yourself. This is a self-help book, but it is also a workbook that I would like you to write in, refer back to, and live with as you begin this journey. When I ask you to do things in the book, please do it when you reach that point. If you delay, it won't have a lasting effect. Spaces are provided within the text to complete tasks assigned to you, and then you can use the supplemental chapter at the end of the book. Links are also provided. Remember, we have to do our homework before we can go outside and play.

My Personal Forgiveness Mantra

My Personal Forgiveness Mantra (continued)

....

....

....

....

....

....

....

....

....

Words Have Power

♡ ◯ ◁   ⊓

Likes 967

One of the reasons a forgiveness mantra is so essential is because words have power. When you speak, you are casting spells on your life. That's why it's called SPELLing. I also believe that we are truly in control of our reality.

There are things I've achieved that sometimes I even think, How the heck did I do that? I mean, I am a brilliant fintech expert from a small town in South Georgia, but there were far more intelligent folks to come out of my hometown than me. What propelled me to the life that I live today? I believed in myself. Even when others laughed at me and doubted me, I trusted and followed my instincts. Notice that I didn't say anything negative about myself? When you read, "I am a brilliant fintech," were you like, "This stuck-up bih . . . ?" Laugh out loud! People are shocked, and it's quite jarring to read or hear someone state positive things about themselves. Folks call you conceited or stuck-up. It's all a setup to keep you from SPELLing the life you desire through your words. And I am not talking about witchcraft. I am talking about how you *feel*. Remember, the brain controls your entire body, so why should you not be concerned with how it makes you feel? If you believe it, then it is so. Please reread that sentence. *If YOU believe it, then it is SO!* Who cares what the hell anyone else thinks or believes?

Be Mindful of Your Financial Mental Health

Likes 9633

In addition to paying careful attention to the words you use daily, you also want to be very mindful of your financial mental health. When you find yourself in a financial storm or experiencing money sickness, I'd like you to start practicing what I call **financial mindfulness**.

According to Merriam-Webster (11th edition), mindfulness is defined as "The quality or state of being conscious or aware of something."

Now, I would like you to take a break.
Go somewhere quiet, close your eyes, and breathe.

Step 1: Breathe in, counting to four slowly. Feel the air enter your lungs.

Step 2: Hold your breath for 4 seconds. Try to avoid inhaling or exhaling.

Step 3: Slowly exhale through your mouth for 4 seconds.

Step 4: Repeat steps one through three until you feel re-centered.

Once you feel centered, I would like you to do the following:

Acknowledge what is going on in your financial life.

a. For example, if it's the first of the month and your car won't start, say to yourself, *"OK, the car won't start, and I have to pay my monthly bills today. I am going to have to do some sort of financial gymnastics to cover the bill to get the car fixed, along with everything else that I have to do. This makes me feel angry and extremely anxious."*

b. Then calmly game out some potential solutions and put together a plan. Do *not* make any reactionary decisions because these are the moments that define your relationship with money.

Instagramification Equals Reactionary Consequences

♡ ◯ ▽   ◻

Likes 9631

How often have we received a bit of bad financial news and immediately jumped to the most extreme solution without thinking it through? This frequently happens for a lot of people. We do this because we've seen our parents and others doing it. We do this because it provides us with immediate gratification, a.k.a. *instagramification*, meaning the stress, anxiety, and angst that go along with the problem disappear immediately (or seemingly so). But to what end? The problem with reactionary decisions is that they're made in the heat of the moment and are not well thought out. And instagramification gets us every time; that's why we all have a love-hate relationship with Amazon. We don't like the way they treat their employees, but we love to press a button and a few hours later, presto! Like magic, we have what we ordered.

Let me give you a real-life example of how a reactionary response to financial decision-making will bite you in the behind every time. When I was still working, I had a married couple as clients who received an IRS letter stating they owed $50,000 in additional taxes after filing with my firm. They received the letter in the summer and instead of calling or emailing me the letter, they freaked out and paid it. The next tax season they came to see me, and I found the letter and canceled check in their paperwork. I asked them why they paid the notice because it wasn't even a bill; it was a proposed assessment. They said the letter scared them, and they just wanted to make the problem go away as quickly as possible. Read that again. *They wanted to make it go away.*

You see, our feelings can fuck up our finances! This is incredibly common. In fact, it's so common that the IRS now routinely sends out these proposed assessments, and many people, like my clients, impulsively pay it to make it go away. Hence, their financial PTSD caused them to make instagramification based on a reactionary decision that wreaked havoc on their finances. If my clients had first taken a break somewhere quiet, practiced the breathing steps to lower their blood pressure, centered themselves, and calmly gamed out potential solutions to the problem, they would not have cashed in their 401(k) to pay the bill that I later discovered they did *not* owe. Yes, you read that correctly. They didn't even owe the damn money!

All we had to do was simply send in a copy of a tax form the IRS already had on file. After I did that, the IRS returned the payment to them. My clients were so thankful, they sent me flowers. But guess what? It was a new tax season, and their reactionary decision to cash in their 401(k) early to pay the bill incurred a tax penalty that they had to pay. So, a new problem to address.

Do you see how reactionary financial decisions can quickly put you in a downward spiral? I say all this to say: no matter the situation, you can take a few minutes or sleep on it before making a financial decision. Even folks who have received an eviction letter or a foreclosure notice have thirty damn days to respond. When we make these rash decisions, we cause a mess of other problems that ripple into waves of chronic financial anxiety and stress.

Straightaway, I already know what you must be thinking. How the hell do you know so much about how the brain works and psychology? Well, I have been with my husband for over twenty years, and I firmly believe that people married to physicians learn as much about their spouse's medical career as they do. Please recognize that *we* are often the ones who help them study for their exams whilst in medical school and thereafter. So, I have earned my MrsMD, so much so that I acquired a trademark for the word.

Throughout our marriage, I learned that dopamine is the pleasure chemical in the brain, so if you are already financially depressed or anxious, a boost of dopamine makes you *feel* like you are happy. Ain't that a blip? It tricks you into thinking that things like shopping make you happy. And trust me, the marketing and advertising firms know this all too well.

Some of the financial decisions we make every day self-sabotage us because we keep chasing that dopamine boost, not unlike a person suffering from substance abuse addiction. We know good and darn well that we shouldn't do these things. We know we don't *need* them. But we allow that little devilish voice in the back of our heads to use our emotions to play us time and time again. And we enjoy that momentary boost of dopamine from making those purchases. Of course, the dopamine comes at a tremendous cost. And trust me, the devil will come to collect it in thirty days, long after the dopamine has worn off. Do you know what is also jacked up? Associating those purchases with the feeling of happiness—also the work of that little devilish voice. Dopamine *does* make you feel happy, but not for long.

Dopamine is like a payday loan. These are loans that have usurious and, in some cases, illegally high interest rates. The loans are given between paydays to help the borrower cover expenses until their next payday. In addition to the extremely high interest rates, payday loans trap many borrowers in a cycle of paying only the minimum fee weekly, because they can never financially cover the principal balance of the loan. Those sneaky payday loans make you feel instantly better because you can cover your expenses, but soon (and *very* soon) you're hit with those usurious fees, and you realize that it wasn't all it was cracked up to be. Dopamine only provides a *temporary mood boost*.

Intrinsic Rewards

Likes 3434

A better way to boost your mood is to increase your serotonin levels. To do this, you can exercise, get some sun, or simply remember the good times in your life. Take your behind for a walk on a sunny day and think about a happy time in your life. Do some yoga or cardio. I also recommend you start celebrating your financial wins, and I don't mean *only* when you get a raise or win some money. I mean, commend yourself when you drive by the fast-food restaurant and go home and make dinner instead. Rejoice when you realize that you have met your monthly savings goal. Jubilate because you decided to buy this book and are making a meaningful change in your life. If you celebrate the small wins, your brain will keep you on the path to financial freedom. These small behavioral changes will train your brain to stop craving those expensive dopamine boosts.

And listen, I understand that it's not easy to change your behavior overnight. I live with depression and anxiety and have to push myself to do nearly everything when life gets really bad for me. It's tough. I understand that it is *not* possible to simply snap your fingers and voilà, things are magically better. This process takes practice, which is why CB4UB includes a 30-day detox plan and why I keep saying it's a way of life—a practice that becomes a habit.

Stop Faking It 'Til You Make It

Likes 3626

Fake it 'til you make it is one of the most toxic mindsets I have ever witnessed. You are literally hiding who you are to fit into some SocieTHEY-imposed image of counterfeit success. Think about how much energy goes into perpetuating a false reality day in and day out. I am exhausted from just typing that, much less living a double life. Not to mention, think about the damage faking it does to your brain. You are unknowingly training your brain to reject who you genuinely are in hopes of becoming something that a marketing firm created. And the kicker is, since you are so busy putting all your energy into faking it, you may never make it.

Faking it 'til you make it is not always about feigning an image of success. It's most commonly associated with our mental health. As a Black woman, I was taught from an early age that I had to be "tough as iron and sharp as steel." That left little room for my humanity. I was taught that vulnerability and emotion were equated with weakness, and there was no place for that in the life of a proper, young Black lady. So, every time I experienced a genuine emotional human response, I thought something was deeply wrong with me. I thought I was crazy for crying when I was sad or for even feeling sad, for that matter. This is extremely problematic programming. You shouldn't punish yourself for having normal reactions to the ups and downs of life. All emotions are valid; it's just how we behave when feeling those emotions.

Whether you are faking that you are happy all the time or faking that you are balling out of control, it makes no difference to your brain. It's all wrong and dangerous. I have a very personal example of how dangerous faking your mental health can be.

On *That Show,* I was forced into sharing that David and I had suffered several miscarriages. Rather than being met with support and understanding, the other women on the show immediately gaslighted me. All while they continuously hurled a seemingly prescribed amount of support and love on another woman who had (thank God) beaten breast cancer almost twenty years prior, yet she brought it up every five minutes. No one said to her, "You should be over that by now." There was also a total lack of support from those in a position to right the wrong. The social media backlash caused me to have one of the worst depressions in my life. Having to endure the cruelty of those women telling me to simply move past the deaths of our children, not to mention people on social media who lacked empathy, was just too much for my heart to bear. I felt like I was in an alternate universe. And the pressure to suck it up and fake it was a bona fide recipe for disaster. Ultimately, the helplessness I felt turned into despair, and a belief that I just didn't want to live in a world so cruel anymore. Yes, it got that bad.

One day, I asked my husband if I would ever be happy again. I truly didn't feel it was possible. He said that I would, and it was perfectly fine for me not to be happy all the time. Reread that sentence, y'all. *It is perfectly fine NOT to be happy all the time.* No one says this! We have all these societal pressures to suck it up and move past horrific traumas in our lives. And yet, you can't just suck it up and snap out of it. Pretending to be perfect all the damn time is so antiquated. It keeps you from living a fulfilling life.

I said it once, and I'll say it again: we are humans, not robots! And no one living with a soul should aspire to be a robot. *We must deal with trauma in our own time and our own way.* When we rush to sweep it under the rug and project a false image of strength or extreme wealth and success, we deny our mind the time to process and heal. And that denial of time and healing can manifest itself in your life in highly destructive ways. Unhealed trauma births that little devilish voice in the back of our heads. The little devil exists because we didn't give our brain enough time to heal, so it sneaks in and takes over. This causes us to make irrational financial (and other) decisions that we would ordinarily not make. CB4UB teaches us to acknowledge that voice and to do the homework.

And you wonder why folks want you to shut up and fake it? It's likely because they haven't dealt with their own traumas. The people I encountered on *That Show* had financial reasons, and they likely did it out of pure jealousy. But, others do it because SocieTHEY wants you to think that something is wrong with you if you aren't smiling, laughing, and jet-setting like all the people in commercials and ads.

Trust me, things will get better when you acknowledge that you are human. We all have triggers, and that's OK. If you falter, be kind to yourself. Check yourself with empathy and compassion. Remember, meaningful change takes time. Meditate and project love, kindness, health, and strength. It is OK to fuck up. Honey chile, I do it every day. As long as you learn from the situation and self-correct, things will be fine. Remember, we create our own reality. Dopamine and serotonin are dopamine and serotonin. The boost you get from taking a walk in the sunlight is the same as the boost you get from buying an expensive pair of shoes. And walking in the sun costs you only your time, while making that unnecessary purchase may cost you your peace of mind.

CHAPTER 2

What Had Happened Was . . .

● ●

IT'S TIME TO CONFESS. I mentioned earlier that you would be required to state in detail the cause of your current financial mess. This is the most important step of CB4UB. I refer to this statement as the #whathadhappenedwas. Since I have no shame, and nor should you, I have included my #whathadhappenedwas.

I thought I truly had it going on. My grammy used to say that I thought I was the cat's meow. And I did. I bought my first house when I was nineteen years old. Correction, I had my first house built when I was nineteen years old. I worked in the family business and was being groomed to take it over. I started a mortgage brokerage firm that covered my monthly expenses. Not to mention, I was still in college. I saved 80 percent of the money I earned from the family business and played with the other 20 percent. I owned a beater car and resisted the temptation to buy a new car even though I could afford one. **Afford** is one of the first of many dangerous words that we will discuss later in this book. I liked investing my money and loved the thought of earning money while I slept, a concept my Uncle Tim taught me when I was young. Life was great! I worked hard, had a good bit of money in the bank, and was still making decent grades. What could go wrong?

Now, I can't blame what happened to me on anyone or any one occurrence. It was a series of jacked-up, incredibly naive, and just plain bad decisions on my part. For starters, I fell in love with "Sam," or at least I thought I did. I ought to use his real damn name, but nope, I have amassed too many assets, and I am sure his ass is still broken and miserable. Sam was ten years my senior and a textbook $50,000-a-year millionaire. Let me stop lying. That fool was probably more like a $30,000-a-year millionaire. He lived life well above his means by conning others out of their hard-earned money. I come from an incredibly loving and supportive family that lives comfortably. My family is not filthy rich, contrary to popular belief. They are all hardworking and have created lives for themselves and their kids for which they can be proud. I sometimes struggle with guilt because of my privilege. And because of this, I sometimes feel that when someone outside my wonderful family shows me love, I must return the favor in the form of payment. That's crappy, right? But a lot of people feel this way whether they come from a family like mine or not.

Sam wasn't even all that. I am an introvert, and I didn't like to go out. I went to class, worked in the family business, did my homework, spent time with the family, slept, and started the loop all over again. I didn't have time to meet anyone, so, of course, I met him at my uncle's office. That was the first red flag. I clearly have daddy issues (from the lack of presence of my biological father. My stepdad, who came into my life when I was an adult, is fantastic). So, what had happened was, I bought this mug a car, gave him a job at my mortgage brokerage firm, and became a paymaster. I don't even recognize the person that I used to be. Did I mention that I caught his arse driving the car I bought for him with the top down and another broad in it? Of course, I blocked him in the intersection, kicked him out of my car, left the car I was driving in the middle of the road, and drove off with her in it. That's a story for another day. Hey, I was young. Needless to say, the woman was uninjured and just a little frightened. I provided his lazy and ungrateful behind with waaaay too many damn benefits for what I received in return. I also became a victim of what I now call **codependent poverty**. I'll tell you about that later, but, basically, I became a human ATM machine for everyone, and I do mean *everyone* around me! I think folks could see it in my eyes or smell my naivete like an expensive perfume.

The Little Devilish Voice Has Entered the Chat

Likes 8226

I started noticing that all the people I've helped—clients, family members, and friends—always looked so nice. With new clothes and hair done, it seemed as if they were always fresh from some fabulous trip, and I looked awful. I was a full-time student who worked full-time for the family business, and I still had to find time to run my little side business that had become very successful. But I didn't have any time for myself.

I was tired constantly, my grades were suffering, business exploded, and I couldn't keep up with the pace. I started to hear that little voice within say, "It seems like everyone else is living the good life, and I look awful and never have any fun. It's just not fair!" So, (there is that word again—remember, I warned you) in addition to being a human ATM, I stopped living my life the way I always had by working hard and saving money. To rebel, I began to live the life that I felt I deserved. Oh, **deserve**—another dangerous word to delete from your daily vernacular.

The Rich Bih Show

Likes 8853

No one could tell me anything! I was flying to London every month to get my hair done by one of the world's top hair extension artists. Yes, I rocked extensions back when only the truly wealthy had them. I can remember being late for a statistics final because a fire at Gatwick Airport in England delayed my flight. Luckily, my professor thought it was funny that I was late for an exam because I had gone to London to get my hair done, so I was able to take it the next day. But what the heck was I thinking scheduling a hair appointment overseas during finals? I bought so many shoes that Imelda Marcos would've been jealous. I had the latest this and the newest that, and I found myself with no savings and a lot of useless crap. More importantly, my jet-setting ways also caused me to lose the momentum and success of my mortgage business because of neglect. Of course, when the money was gone, the man I thought I loved left me as well. I became extremely depressed and found the only way to make myself *feel* temporarily happy was to spend more. Sound familiar?

The Rich Bih Show Is Canceled

Likes 2365

So, what had happened was . . . I woke up one day and decided to make a change. A real change, not a faux change like we fool ourselves into saying we will do each year around New Year's Eve. I knew that it would be difficult—and painful. I was going to be jealous of everyone else around me who seemed to have it all, but I had to keep my eye on the prize— being in control of my financial future the way I used to be. I wanted to be completely out of debt and save at least two years of my annual expenses. Yes, you read that correctly. You need two years saved before you can breathe a sigh of relief knowing that you have your life in order. The average time someone is unemployed these days is over a year and a half. That's a long freaking time to be unemployed! I don't mean just underemployed, like when you take a job in which you earn less than you had before. I mean completely jobless. And we know unemployment income is a joke these days and constantly under fire, so I believe to be truly free, you need to have a minimum of what I call "what it costs to be you" put away for a minimum of two years.

For example, between rent, utilities, food, fuel, and other miscellaneous expenses, let's say it costs you $2,000 per month to be you. This means you will need $2,000 x 24 months = $48,000. And that's a minimum of $48,000 that will need to be socked away and invested to make you feel like you are truly OK.

You are probably thinking, Well, it was easy for you to get yourself back on track because you had a family business to rely on. Well, you are wrong! It seemed like an almost impossible task at the time. I lost the business that covered my monthly expenses. My family business was suffering because the industry was changing, so I wasn't receiving a paycheck regularly, and I had amassed a ton of credit card debt when I was living the good life. **The good life**—here's another string of horrifically dangerous words that you should banish from your vocabulary. So, in some ways, it was harder for me because at least many of you can depend on a steady paycheck. In a family business, when things go wrong, the family members are the first to go without pay. That's just the way it is.

They say God never puts more on us than we can handle. I used to believe this meant God wanted us to struggle. I rationalized all my failures in this way. I now realize that our trials and tribulations are simply lessons, and they will keep rearing their little heads in our life if we choose not to learn the lesson each time it's taught to us. It's as if we are given the same homework assignment over and over again and instead of doing the homework, we take our behinds outside to play, wondering why we keep getting a failing grade. When you finally do the homework, you will discover that life is *not* about the struggle. It's about truly living the life *you* want. The life I wanted was to retire at the age of forty. I am proud to say I met my goal by a year, and I retired at forty-one.

Now, tag, you're it. Take a moment and think about your #whathadhappenedwas. Why do you find yourself in the financial situation you are in now? Be honest about it. Admitting your faults is the most important part of CB4UB. You must realize and state that you have trouble managing your finances. You can accomplish this in a few ways. You can write it on the pages provided within this book, record a voice memo on your phone, or if you are really 'bout it, you can film a video and upload it to social media using the hashtag #crawlbeforeyouball. Your #whathadhappenedwas is a contract you are making with yourself to join the revolution that is CB4UB and to hold yourself accountable whenever you waver. And trust me, we *all* waver.

If you choose to write your #whathadhappenedwas, please do so in the space provided below. If you need additional space, feel free to use the workbook pages at the end of the book.

CHAPTER 3

Codependent Poverty

> **It's OK to Say No!**

Likes 1896

NOW THAT YOU HAVE your #whathadhappenedwas declaration, it is time to discuss one of the main reasons many of us have a jacked-up relationship with money. I refer to it as **codependent poverty**, which basically means when someone in your family or friend group is chronically monetarily strapped, everyone who helps them out each month will also be.

Have you ever noticed that when you seem to have your stuff together, someone in your family loses their job or can't pay their rent? And who do they call to bail them out? You, naturally! You are the responsible, successful family member, and it is your **duty** to help everyone out. Oh, it is excruciating for me to say these darn words because I worked so hard to eliminate them from my life. **Duty**—another dangerous word. Quit using it today! That word will make you think it's just plain selfish of you not to extend a helping hand to a family member when they are in a time of need. I am here to tell you that it's OK to say "NO."

If you don't learn to say no, you will find that a family member's drama will come around and pull you under every time you have your head above water. It's called perpetuating the cycle of codependent poverty. My own extended family is a prime example. Everyone is in everyone else's business and owes money to each other that will never be repaid. I can remember a time when my extended family members would go out to dinner for a nice family meal, and when the check came, everyone had to go to the bathroom. Or, they would simply keep talking as if they were oblivious, almost with an attitude, like, I know you ain't looking at me to pay that bill. It was expected that the most "well-to-do" family member would foot the bill. When I was younger, that person was my favorite uncle. He was successful and extremely kind. He understood the importance of generational wealth, but he didn't fully grasp the dangers of codependent poverty.

My uncle had a thriving business and a good head on his shoulders. I witnessed firsthand how codependent poverty weighed heavily on him. It seemed that each time he triumphed in business, a family emergency sidelined him. The more successful he became, the more family emergencies popped up. And somehow, he was the only person who could save the day by throwing money at the problem.

People would have been surprised to know he suffered financially because he had agreed to pay the bills of too many family members. He had very little personal debt, but when you are paying for Jerry's car, Caleb's light bill, Lori's dog's monthly vet bills, and Marsha's children's day-care expenses each month, you can't succeed. The codependent pressure to take care of everyone caused him to make some poor life-altering decisions. These were decisions he wouldn't have made had he not felt obligated to carry our entire family on his back.

As I grew older, I realized that I was being groomed to take over his role. I began to notice that when I would go out to dinner with relatives my age and a bit older, I was **expected** to pay the bill. I noticed that I started getting sad calls from certain relatives who could not pay a certain bill each month. After a while, I started paying the bills each month as if they were my own. Do you think any of my relatives called me to say, "Hey, stop making those payments for me each month"? Heck no! After waking up and realizing that I was enabling folks and codependent poverty was destroying my life, I took a stand and decided to break the cycle. My mother has an apt phrase that I love and still use today: *"You can only buy whatever your income and expenses dictate that you can!"*

The keyword here is *your.* Basically, this phrase means not to include others' income or assets into the equation when you are debating a purchase or weighing any other financial decision in your life. A codependent poverty lifestyle fosters the belief that it's all right to claim your sibling or parent's assets as your own. No matter how entitled you think you may be, this mindset is damaging to both you and your family.

So, when you get that call from your younger brother asking you if you think he should buy a motorcycle—run! And feel free to use my momma's saying when faced with this dilemma.

Come-to-Jesus Moment

Likes 2693

Now that you understand that it's OK to say no, it's time for the family to have a come-to-Jesus moment. If you aren't Southern or religious, this simply means putting everything on the table and creating a plan for change, regardless of whose feelings may be hurt. Why can't we talk to our family members about money? Have a family meeting and tell everyone the jig is up. I am out. No more calling me with your financial drama. It's over. Your money problems are not mine. Your failure to plan no longer constitutes an emergency for me. Don't be afraid to speak your truth. You aren't being mean. You are helping them. Can you hear a bit of my pain while reading these words? I can, lol. I saddled myself with this relentless guilt for years, and the day I decided to take care of just Buffie was the day I started living my life.

Enabling vs. Helping

Likes 663

You may feel as though you are abandoning your family after this come-to-Jesus moment, so let's talk about the difference between enabling and helping. I genuinely believe in helping, but enabling is not helping. So now, when a family member calls me for assistance, I give them the opportunity to do some work at one of our businesses to earn the money. If I have a cousin whose house is in foreclosure, I draw up a contractual agreement and detail what services need to be completed within one or more of our businesses. I provide them with a timeline. And so long as they keep up their end of the deal, I keep up the repayment program to the mortgage company. And I always offer work that they can do after hours or on weekends. It's tough, but you have to do what you have to do when you are in a bind. It's truly a win-win situation for both of us. One, I get much-needed work done around the office without feeling like I had to loan my family member any money. And two, my family member doesn't have to resent me because they had to ask me for a loan they know could never be repaid. Now, if you don't have a business, there are always projects around the house, things Grandma needs, or whatever you can think of that provides you both with a benefit that will work.

Some people on social media have commented that I have a transactional relationship with my family members when it comes to money. I don't disagree. When folks post this, it is meant as shade or a slight, but if you ask me to part with my money, that *is* a financial transaction. If you ask me to part with my most valuable asset—my time—that is a time transaction. Sharing the same DNA doesn't matter. And the DNA conversation is the trap. When you start to think of it in this way, you will begin to break free of the codependent poverty lifestyle. You don't owe anyone anything. If you want to help, make it a transactional event. If you wish to continue to enable, make it a familial obligation, a.k.a. codependent poverty.

Friends—How Many of Us Have Them?

Likes 9566

Do you know who else we enable in our lives? Our friends. Some of us are closer to our friends than to our biological family. Remember, we have to do our homework and chores before we can go outside and play. And while we are on the subject of playing, you might have to find different playmates. If your friends aren't supportive of your CB4UB journey, you might have to cut out the playdates until you are strong enough to deal with them. We have all heard the adage "misery (a.k.a. the devil) loves company." Unhappy people sometimes get consolation from knowing that others are unhappy too. You could be making positive changes in your life, but your friends who aren't doing well may try to persuade you to conform to their financial dysfunction; in other words, they cast negative spells on you. When I speak about words having power, some people look at me side-eyed, but if you take the time to think about what I am saying as it relates to your CB4UB journey, you will understand it. If we create our reality and our minds control everything in our bodies, voicing negative things about ourselves can have a damaging effect on our behavior.

Furthermore, being around those who project negativity on us won't help either. If you are in a positive space and surround yourself with positive people, you will be positive. Protect your space. It's so important.

You Just Can't Play with Everybody

Likes 2633

As mentioned earlier, I will be shading some of those broads from *That Show.* I'm going to stick to my word and share a little anecdote from a time in my life when I didn't protect my space. On *That Show,* the ladies and I went out to dinner one night. One of the women was very excited about closing on her new multi-million-dollar home with her husband. She was understandably proud of this achievement, but also because this would be her first time listed on the mortgage with him. She'd worked hard in her career to earn more income and spent years repairing her credit, so this was a significant milestone and financial achievement for her. Since everyone there was supposedly accomplished and believed in the notion of women's empowerment, you'd think she would've been met with support and congratulations.

Nope! These jealous heifers said to this woman, "That's not a big deal; we ALL have homes." One of those broads even added, "I have been on the mortgage with my husband for years. That's nothing."

I was astonished, and the so-called leader of the group never corrected anyone. So, of course, I did, even though I was the new girl and was expected to remain mute. I don't stand for dream killers or purveyors of misery. I said, "Why can't we support her in this new chapter? This is a benchmark event in *her* life, and she doesn't need to be compared to that of yours." The women looked bewildered, because apparently no one ever checks them when they are truly wrong. They gaslighted this woman into making her feel as though her achievement was meaningless, when not one of them owned a two-million-dollar home.

You have to be selective about who you allow into your orbit. You can't play with everybody. The world is full of people who can't stand for anyone who appears to be doing better than they are. I once got bashed on social media and on *Andy Cohen's What Happens Live* for mentioning on *That Show* that it gets lonely at the top. The wolves flipped my words and accused me of believing everyone was beneath me, which was not my point nor what I meant. I'm not even like that! My point was that financial success sometimes comes at a terrible cost—isolation. Money can make people insane, so you must protect your spirit. Understand, the CB4UB journey can get lonely.

Small Amounts Add TF Up

♡ ◯ ◁   ⊓

Likes 1789

The types of people on *That Show* are also the ones who prey on kind individuals. I am always surprised that the people who give the most barely have enough for themselves. There can be various reasons for this generosity. Some people may give because they think, Well, what if I need help? The family member or friend that I help will be there to help me. Well, that's not always the case. We need to get to a place where we don't need outside help with our finances. Sounds like a fairy tale, right? It sounds like such a damn impossibility. Well, I am here to tell you that it's not.

Many students in my digital course break down when discussing codependent poverty. Cash App or other peer-to-peer payment apps that make it easy for folks to send you a request for money whenever the hell they want have a lot of people messed up. The blatant audacity of this freakin' app. Now, I know some of you feel this app has made life convenient for you, but it's also an easy way for your freeloading family members and friends to guilt you out of your coins. It has also made it extremely convenient for Cash App and other peer-to-peer payment apps to sell the info of how and who you lend or give money to each month, but we'll talk about that in my next book.

Friends and family may not realize that the act of requesting small amounts is part of the plan. Small amounts seem innocent. No one asked for thousands of dollars. You were only asked for the amount you may spend on lunch or coffee today. Asking for small amounts of cash is usually not a huge burden for one person. But the thing is, many of them go on to ask nine other people for fifty dollars, and then poof, they have enough to get their hair and nails done. If you're someone who gets frequent requests to give small amounts of money—which on the surface might seem harmless—these small amounts add the fuck up and mess with your financial goals, especially when your goal is to pay your bills and survive.

It's OK to say "NO!" Delete the app and others like it. How many times have you received a text asking, "Can you Cash App me twenty dollars this month?" Add it up, and then take a moment to process how much of that money you could have saved and invested in yourself. Why is it deemed selfish to take care of yourself? And what will happen when they Cash App you into the poor house or when someone in the family has a real emergency? Ain't nobody thinking about that possibility. This codependent poverty trap is why most people can't seem to get their shit together.

Time Vampires

Likes 6989

Please don't get me started with family and friends' rampant abuse of a far more valuable asset than your money—*your time*! How often have you been asked to babysit without receiving even a thank you, much less a coin? They tell you they only need you for a few hours and show the hell up two days later as if you had nothing else to do with your life. Or, "Can you teach me how to set up a business?" And you set time aside, and they don't even show up? How about, "Can you get your friend to hook me up with XYZ?" then you beg your friend to help the family member, and your cousin blows the whole thing off? Oh, child, sometimes I'd rather part with the coin than waste my damn time. It's time, pun intended, to stop the time snatchers.

The breakdowns in my digital course come when my students face the ugly truth that they did, in fact, have money they could've saved. Instead of investing it, they invested in whatever familial or friend emergency that conveniently popped up throughout the year. One of my students shared with the group, her eyes filled with tears, that she constantly bailed out her family members, and not one of them, and I mean none of them, ever bothered to call and ask how she was doing. That shit pisses me off. Folks don't even have enough respect to finesse the situation with a "How are you doing?" text before asking you to part with your hard-earned money. Just plain disrespectful! She went on to say that she is an empath and felt she *had* to help them. My husband, Dr. David Purselle, interrupted a Zoom call to say one of the most profound things that I have ever heard him say:

> *"You can have empathy for others and relate to what they are going through without opening your wallet. It's NOT your job to fix everything. You can love your family members and friends and show them compassion by simply listening to them."*

She burst into tears. It was so quiet on the Zoom call filled with two hundred people. The realization that it is not their job to fix everything started to resonate. My students were beginning to get IT. And, I hope by sharing this story with you that you are beginning to get IT too. Stop being the fixer for everyone, and work on fixing your own situation first. You're not helping anyone if you keep compromising yourself financially. And if all else fails, blame me. Say you are crawling right now. You invested in this book and possibly my course, and you have to go through the steps. Let them be mad at me. I can take it. :)

If You Just Can't Go Cold Turkey

Likes 348

Now, I am not an evil, coldhearted, uncaring person. Really, I am not. Because I am a bit of a softy, I came up with a great way to deal with those inevitable family calls. It's something that none of them ever knew, but it helped me to deal mentally and financially with money and family. It's the crawling approach to just saying no. This will help you ease your way into the no.

Here's a little story. I had a young lady come to my office for tax prep. As I looked through her paperwork, I noticed she had had a significant raise from last year's wages. She'd earned around $65,000 the previous year and over $98,000 in the current. I congratulated her. She looked sad, so, naturally, I asked why. She told me no one would ever know she earned that kind of money. She said there was less than twenty-five dollars in her checking account and six more days until payday. "Thank God you can take your fee out of my tax refund because I wouldn't even be able to pay you today," she remarked.

I asked if I could be frank with her, and she agreed. "Quit giving your family all your money," I piped out.

"How in the world did you know?" She looked at me as if I were an oracle.

"Girl, I was you ten years ago." And I was!

I then recommended she develop a monthly budget. She said she had a budget, but her mom called her two weeks ago and asked to borrow/give her $750 to fix her car. A few days later, her dad needed $325 to pay his credit card bill. I interrupted her and asked, "Aren't both of your parents living in your house and on social security?" I already knew the answer because I'd prepared her taxes and their taxes. She said, "Yes." I then asked her why it was imperative to fix her mom's car. She looked at me like I was a crazy woman. I went on to point out that her mom didn't have a job to get to each day, and her dad's car worked just fine. I mean, these are not life-threatening reasons to just keep giving up your money.

I told her how to deal with family/friends and money. Allocate a certain amount of money each month that you can live without comfortably. Don't include this amount in your budget if you don't include monthly savings. So, if there is *no* extra money and you aren't saving, skip ahead to "Some Mo' Options." In her case, she could set aside $500 per month comfortably after meeting her financial responsibilities, including savings. I told her not to tell her mom and dad because then, miraculously, every month, they would **need** (yet another dangerous word) $500. Now, each month, when her mom asks her for twenty dollars for gas, she can give it to her, but she must remember to mentally withdraw that amount from the $500 per month allocated for her. I told her to say to herself, "She is down to $480." When her requests exceed the $500, she can then say "NO" without feeling guilty. And maybe there will be a few months in which her mother's requests will not exceed the amount set aside for her.

Some Mo' Options

Likes 2564

In our family, codependent poverty became so cumbersome that I came up with the idea of creating a private family bank for my immediate family members. The Rockefeller family did this, as they had so much damn wealth that they didn't need banks, so they created their own. Now, I know you are crawlin' and ain't ready for a damn family bank. But give me a moment to convince you that you may want to start one for your family as a savvy investment strategy and a way to really help. There are many ways this can be accomplished. One of the most common ways is to leverage overfunded whole life insurance policies. Basically, if a family member wants to start a business, buy a car, or needs a couple hundred bucks to cover an unexpected expense, they can take a loan against the whole life insurance policy to cover the expense. Of course, this loan would be paid back over time. And since you or a family member are borrowing against yourself, no one cares about credit or any of the usual underwriting stipulations. You determine that yourself.

We also established a family microcredit club. When someone in the family requests a small loan, we developed a formal process for them to apply. They submit their request to the family board. To keep everything fair, we hired a firm, a.k.a. employees, to handle these matters, so that family members don't know who is or isn't using the system. The folks who invest in it do so like any other investment. And the family members who need to use the service do so without embarrassment. There are several amazing pros about the club that I created for my big, extended family, but this can work for a small family as well:

1. It's an excellent investment. The risk/reward is different because it's your family. Even if we lose money, we also lose the constant "Can you loan me money?" texts. When asked, you can say, "I invested in the family microcredit club, so you should apply there." And boom! Your conscience is clear. You're also not negating their needs, just referring them to a more responsible way of borrowing money.
2. Variables like personal credit and all that are thrown out the window. The board develops the criteria to lend.
3. If someone fails to repay, then they are kicked out of the club until they pay the loan back, plus interest and fees. Consequences are a good thing!
4. We also report their payment history to the credit bureaus to help them rebuild their traditional credit.

It's really not too difficult a thing to do. Have a meeting with those family members who get hit up every month and develop the business from there. It has worked out well for us.

The Isolation Is Only Temporary

Likes 2094

It's not easy to break free from a codependent-poverty family lifestyle. You will be ostracized. You will notice that you aren't invited to as many family functions anymore. Folks will say you've changed and are "acting funny" now that you have money. Be patient with their progress. They will eventually come around when they begin their own financial journey. It's all part of the process. My cousin told me recently that he was angry with me for a couple of years because I refused to loan him $1,500. He has since gotten his financial life in order and is now the person folks constantly hit up. He told me he now understands why I said no and is currently working to create those boundaries with his sibling and mother.

Taking yourself *out* of that lifestyle is so freeing. You will immediately notice that you're less stressed and have time and money to do the things that *you* want to do with your life. And that's OK!

CHAPTER 4

Check Yo'self with Empathy!

● ●

OK, FIRST, LET ME SAY that I am proud of you for deciding to change your life! Now, let's be real with each other—you are going to have to check yourself throughout this process. By that, I mean you will have to block out *all* the social and familial influences that cause you to make awful financial decisions. This can be a struggle. You will also need to develop empathy for yourself. Don't be surprised if you screw up; we all do. And that's OK. You need to periodically remind yourself that no one is perfect (despite what you see on TV and social media). We are all a work in progress, which is a good thing. Complacency—believing you know every damn thing and have no room to grow or learn—is the work of the devil. So, if you faltered, simply dust yourself off and pick yourself up again with compassion. Count it as a lesson learned and move the fuck on.

This book is called *Crawl Before You Ball* for a reason. When you begin to crawl, it's important to reward yourself for your efforts. So while you are on your CB4UB journey, build into your budget some fun for yourself and your family. I liken this to the risk/reward spectrum in investing. The most important investment you will ever make is in yourself. So reward yourself from time to time. It will also give your brain an incentive to continue. No one wants to sacrifice and never see the fruits of their labor. You will likely not make it if you omit this step. Now, I am not saying go out and blow your savings or do anything crazy. What I am saying is you should budget for some of the pleasures that you will likely cut out while you are crawling. Reward yourself, your spouse, and your kids periodically, and you will still be able to achieve your goals. You know they do this at casinos, right? They let you win a little to give you a boost of dopamine to keep you gambling and parting with your coins. Instead of allowing corporations, sharks, marketing companies, and other wolves in sheep's clothing to take advantage of this knowledge of how the brain actually functions, you should too.

Get Yo' Mind Right

Likes 84849

Step 1: **Get your mind right**. To properly check yourself, you must first reprogram your mind. We are brainwashed into thinking we **deserve** this and desperately **need** that. Yet, in actuality, what we need to survive is minimal. I remember watching the documentary *Babies* and marveling that no matter the parent's socioeconomic status, all the babies featured had their basic needs met. In fact, each baby appeared happy and healthy. The documentary featured several families, but the two that made the biggest impression on me were a financially wealthy family from Japan and a financially poor family from Namibia. Notice that I mentioned the families were either financially wealthy or financially poor, because you can be wealthy or poor in ways other than money.

The Namibian baby lived in a hut, and the family made use of the things around them in ways that some of us couldn't even imagine. For example, they didn't have extravagances like disposable diapers, so when the baby needed to potty, he just did it out in the open, old-school commando style. You know how our parents used to allow us to run around the house naked, and we ended up going number two on Mommy's new couch? When the child finished, his mother simply picked up a piece of leftover corn on the cob from the previous night's dinner and cleaned his little bottom with it. The baby didn't even have toys—in the traditional sense, that is. There is a scene where the baby is looking for something to play with, and he finds a pebble on the ground. He smiles as he throws it in the air and catches it for hours. The baby was so happy, and it truly warmed my heart.

Conversely, the sweet little girl from Japan had an entire room filled with toys yet seemed annoyed because every toy she picked up bored her. If that little boy could be so happy playing with a pebble, why can't we?

The Harsh Truth Whilst Getting Yo' Mind Right

Likes 9844

We can learn a lot from that happy child playing with the pebble. The reality is we don't *need* that much to be happy in this life. It's our societally influenced, ever-evolving wants that are the real problem. It's time for a big and loud yet loving sister moment to help you reshape your financial mentality. Some of y'all are about to become angry with me. The following statements may seem severe, but their presentation in this way is a vital part of the wake-up call that is CB4UB.

You Shouldn't Have Some of Your *Ish*—#periodt

Please repeat aloud the following sentences as you read them:

- If you aren't bringing in eight figures per year, you should be flying commercial, not private. #periodt

- If you don't have a credit card with enough credit to book your flight and hotel room, you shouldn't be taking a trip to the Maldives or anywhere else. #periodt

- If you just borrowed twenty dollars from your brother for gas, you shouldn't be wearing Louboutin shoes, a.k.a. red bottoms. #periodt

---

- If you have no intentions of going camping for three straight months on the most dangerous terrain in the world, you don't need to shop at expensive-arse REI for gear and clothing. (This one is for all the Dr. David Purselles out there.) #periodt

- If you are paying rent to someone, you shouldn't be driving a luxury vehicle. #periodt

- If you are in your late fifties, on a reality TV show, and just bought or are renovating your house, you should stop buying labels. #periodt (I told you I would shade those broads, and I am a woman of my word!)

The Wealth Mindset

Likes 4456

Now, let's talk about wealth because we *really* need to do so. These reality TV shows, like the one I was on, have confused everyone about wealth. And that is by design, of course. TV is funded by advertising, and advertisers want you to part with your coins so you can be like your favorite reality personalities. One reason I agreed to do a stint on reality TV was to prove that our aspirational lives are actually attainable.

When I was being considered for *That Show*, I actually played into those stereotypes. I wore designer labels when we filmed prior to my casting, all while knowing I would not be doing so once I was on the show. After being cast, I came to the office to meet the team. One of the higher-ups asked me, "Do you dress like this every day?"

I smiled and said, "Yes, I do."

He then said, "But when we filmed before, you had a flashier sense of style." I smiled again and signed my paperwork.

Too often, all you are permitted to see on television are people who live very aspirational lives in mansions, drive luxury vehicles, and wear costly labels. We all know this is a recipe for financial disaster. Just think about the medium of television; it's based primarily on what you see. It's difficult to depict a lifestyle without falling into the trappings that I listed before. But I was on a mission, whether they realized it or not. I was on a mission to change the narrative.

As a friend on *That Show*, I was asked to host a party at my home so the cast and viewers could get to know me. The show already had many other women, so this was the only way to make my mark. Production tends to help cast members who are lost with what to do, but I am Buffie, so that was not needed. They wanted me to hire a party planner and film it. I declined. I said, "I never hire party planners. I plan my own parties. That is a waste of money." No shade to party planners, but I am type A—organized and with a Rolodex of clients as vendors—so I didn't need their help. Shade moment: I noticed they didn't have any problem showing Kathy Hilton on the *Real Housewives of Beverly*

Crawl Before You Ball

Hills planning her own parties, but I can only surmise why she was depicted accurately, and I was not.

I invited the cast to my annual "Fab and Frugal" party. This event is typically only for my clients, family, and friends (shade). It is a way to show the people in my orbit that I practice what I preach. The party is to celebrate the end of tax season and show that we can rock fabulously frugal fashions without breaking the bank. We don't need to wear our assets on our asses. I offered a $1,000 prize to the person who had the most fabulous and frugal outfit. The total budget for outfits in years past was significantly lower than the one I set for the taping, because some of the women on *That Show* just can't dress without wearing labels (more shade). So, I set the budget at $500 total for the outfit, including accessories, shoes, bag, and other accoutrements. Some of the ladies liked the challenge and went for it. Some didn't. If you watched the episode, you know what I mean. If you didn't, I will enlighten you.

Our Atlanta home is in one of the most prestigious neighborhoods in the city. The street we live on is especially remarkable. So, of course, this was a lovely party filled with Atlanta's movers and shakers. Some of the people at the party were worth hundreds of millions of dollars and kept to the budget guidelines without groaning or pitching a fit. But, of course, some of the nouveau-riche Bravolebrities lost their damn minds. Some even pretended they had to go out and purchase something to wear because everything in their closet was so very expensive. You can't make this shit up. I felt sorry for them and still do. Well, no, I don't. I will say it again, "Wealth whispers and money jingles, jangles, and screams."

Anyway, back to the folks who didn't get it. Half of the ladies showed up in nice dresses or jumpsuits and stayed within budget. Some showed up in obviously cheap attire to mock what I was trying to do, and then felt embarrassed when they saw that everyone else understood the assignment. Of course, all my friends, clients, family, and uber-wealthy neighbors looked amazing and were excited about the contest, being on the show, and attending the party. The youngest lady in the cast made the best effort. Someone else wore jeans. The doctor on the reality show, firmly within Satan's grasp, looked like she was going to a strip club. The vilest one looked all right but kept commenting negatively on how cheap her dress was (likely due to her embarrassment), while the other two ladies made an honest effort. The youngest cast member was a finalist in the contest, and I appreciated her participation and understanding the assignment. She looked amazing as usual. After we all cast our votes, one of my clients won. She had made her dress, and it fit her like a glove.

My point is that even in a beautiful mansion in Buckhead, with fancy people and champagne popping, we could all look stunning without breaking the bank. I wanted to teach folks to invest in appreciating assets like a home, instead of investing in expensive clothing labels that depreciate the minute you wear them. This would give viewers hope that they can attain the things their favorite star is wearing without going into debt. This was an important message for me to impart to viewers. So important, in fact, that during my entire season on the show, I decided to wear only what "regular folks" wore—clothing from fast fashion companies that looked great! I never wore anything that cost more than $250 (shoes, outfit, bag, everything) the entire season. And I was on every episode except two, so that was a lot of clothing. I can only imagine what those women's wardrobe budgets looked like. And to each her own. I am different and highlighting that difference is good TV.

After each episode, I posted my outfit and the cost. I even grew my social media following by doing so instead of posting the typical, meaningless cute pics of myself wearing labels (even more shade). I think some of these networks miss the mark when promoting aspirational lives because they rarely depict tangible lifestyles. They are slowly beginning to see the benefit of casting *real* characters on these shows whom viewers can relate to.

All right, now that you've gotten a taste of "reality tea" and my TV PTSD, it's time to get back to work. To get yo' mind right, you need to truly understand what the hell wealth actually is. Let's first get into the different types of wealth that all financial experts typically agree on:

1. Financial wealth, a.k.a. coins
2. Social wealth, a.k.a. human connection and support
3. Time wealth, a.k.a. freedom

4. Health wealth, a.k.a. mind, body, and soul

CB4UB helps you address all four types of wealth by focusing primarily on numbers one and four: your mental health wealth and financial wealth. Your concept of wealth may vary from someone else's. For example, social wealth might mean continuing the tradition of a Sunday family dinner. Family support and connectedness are powerful forms of social wealth. Not everyone has that. Having people you can rely upon for support is incredibly important and a blessing.

Creating fun and happy family memories together is definitely a dopamine boost. Whenever I talk about my success in business, I am occasionally met with skepticism, like the following: "Well, it was easy for you to become successful because your family has money." Nothing could be further from the truth. I never took any money from my family. I had a college scholarship, and when I lost it because I was busy running my businesses and not studying, I paid my own tuition. I am telling you this for a reason. Skeptics like to point out that I was born on third base. And I agree but not because of my family's financial wealth. I was born on third base and hit a home run in the game of life because of my family's *social* wealth. Having people I could depend on was far better than having access to money. Even if you have financial difficulties and your family is unable to help you monetarily, knowing they'll be there for you is the best form of wealth.

If you've been blessed with the ability to work one job, work from home, or not trade your time for money, thus allowing you time to be with your family, this constitutes a type of wealth—time wealth. Time is the scarcest resource of all. Just as land is scarce, so is time. A positive outcome from the tragedy of COVID-19 is that it forced companies to realize that many of their employees can do their jobs efficiently from home. If you've been blessed with this gift of time wealth, a.k.a. freedom, then be in the spirit of gratitude. I know so many financially wealthy people who would trade places with you any day because they rarely get to see their families. Remember what I said before? No one actually *wants* to work all the damn time.

Lifestyle Marketing—Don't Fall for the Okey Doke

Likes 4448

We always envision the wealthy as people who live like rock stars. Well, I'll let you in on a little secret: the only people who ball out of control and live like rock stars *are* rock stars! And most of the time, they don't even have to pay for their lavish trips, stints at local nightclubs, and shopping sprees. Companies give them all that swag. So, wake up! It's all deceptive marketing. Don't try to mimic their behavior. It's a trick.

The best show to illustrate this new form of advertising is ABC's *Black-ish*. It's done in a rather ingenious way. The father character, played by Anthony Anderson, works for an advertising agency. So, when the show needs to advertise a new car brand, they simply act like he is coming up with a pitch as part of his job. He will drive the car home, and his kids and wife will try it out. All the while stretching the traditional thirty-second ad into an entire scene on the show. And we typically don't fast-forward through those scenes. Subliminally, we now want that car because our favorite characters have that car. When we see footage of Beyoncé and Blue Ivy shopping at Target, we think, Oh, if it's good enough for Bey, then . . . Do you really believe Beyoncé goes to a damn Target to shop with her child? No. Safety issues alone would stop me, but trust and believe Bey was paid in Target equity for that footage.

A Come-to-Jesus Moment for Couples

Likes 9098

If you are married, dating, shacking up, hanging out, or whatever you call it, if your finances are commingled with another person, you've got to sit and talk with your partner. CB4UB will not work if only one party is making the change. You *both* have to commit to the program to have success. This may be a deal-breaker for some of you. Financial difficulties are the number one reason for divorce in this country, so check with your partner and work it out now! When I used to host my annual financial interventions, I wouldn't allow folks to attend who were married or cohabitating unless each party agreed to begin the new CB4UB way of life.

Full transparency is very important in a healthy relationship. In addition to joint savings and investment accounts, you will need to agree to have one joint bank account for all household expenses. Nothing else should come out of that account. Nowadays, auto-draft billing makes this fairly easy to do. Then each of you will get a weekly or monthly allowance to be deposited into your separate but equal personal accounts.

If you are a dual-income household, it might be time to think about living on one of your incomes and investing the other person's income. Yes, you read that correctly. Dave and I have done this for years. And guess which income we live off? The one who earns the least. If you can do this for a specific time, you will amass enough in savings and investments to one day live off the interest and passive income earned from those investments; then, you can both stop trading your time for money and quit working and start living. How else do you think I was able to retire at forty-one? That's the best way to keep the budget straight and to get yo' mind right about CB4UB as a couple. Now, if you can't afford to live on one income or you're not a dual-income family, consider some incentives, such as a couple's saving's competition. Who can save the most? The loser could be tasked with doing chores around the house. Or, whoever saves the most could earn an extra twenty dollars per pay period. Competition can be fun in marriage and a heck of an incentive. Small amounts add up!

Chirren, a.k.a. Children

Likes 6986

If you have kids, you need to have a talk with them. The entire family has to be on board for this way of life to work. If not, children, more so than a partner, will derail your plans because it's so darn hard to say no to their cute little faces! I suggest you sit them down and discuss why you are deciding to make these changes. For example, tell the kids that Mommy and Daddy want to save money for a down payment on a new house. Explain the benefits of homeownership to your kids. Don't dumb it down. Just break it down for them. Though they may not like the idea of forgoing a new Xbox game every week, you will be teaching them a valuable financial lesson. Include the kids' allowances in your budget and get them to make the *Crawl Before You Ball* pledge as well.

My Nephew Learns a Valuable Lesson

A cool thing my family did for my nephews was set up prepaid debit cards for them. The cards are linked to my and my husband's account, my sister's, and my mom and dad's account, so that we can add money when we want and track their spending habits. Ten-year-old Jalen and eight-year-old Aiden know all about saving and the power of compound interest. We basically sat them down one day and explained how you can earn money by not spending your money and leaving it in a high-yield savings account. I remember their little eyes were as big as saucers when they realized what we meant.

One day while shopping, a funny scenario unfolded with Aiden, my younger nephew. He had recently received fifty dollars from us all for bringing home a perfect report card. Aiden decided to do a little shopping. He bought a used game and went to the movies a few times and bought popcorn. My sister, Courtney, took him to Walmart one day, and he picked up a few more things. As he pulled out his wallet, Courtney asked him if he had enough money left on his card and he said, "Yes." He didn't, and she knew that he didn't, but we had already discussed as a family to allow this scenario to play out when it came up. Aiden marched up to the register, swiped his debit card, and typed in his PIN. He then said to the cashier, "Ten dollars cashback, please." The lady smiled and commented on how adorable he was. Her smile soon turned to a frazzled look when she had to tell him that his card was declined. Aiden told the cashier that could not be possible, and my sister laughed. He looked up at her. "Mommy, fix it—make it work!"

Courtney asked the people in line behind them if they cared if she discussed this issue with her son, and they all said it was fine. Courtney asked Aiden if he had been keeping track of his spending. He said yes and rattled off the items that he'd already purchased to this point and the cost. My sister asked him to subtract those expenses from the fifty dollars that he had earned for his good grades. Aiden frowned and said, "But I thought Auntie Buffie and Mrs.

Evers [a.k.a. his grandmother] would just keep adding money to my card for me when it ran out!" My sister laughed and told Aiden that they would call Auntie Buffie after they checked out. She made Aiden give his items back; she did *not* buy them for him. When they got home, they called me, and I had a long talk with Aiden about how money is *earned* and how he shouldn't expect people to just give it to him. I also explained to him that he shouldn't count what I have as if it were his. Aiden was embarrassed, but he learned a valuable lesson that day.

Now, some of you may think it was harsh to make that little boy put everything back. Why didn't his mom just pay for it all? My answer is that life is sometimes harsh, and what better time for him to learn this lesson than the present? Learning how to budget, save, and sacrifice is a learned skill for children and should become part of their lives. Kids only know what is normal for their life. Make CB4UB a part of their new normal, and they will adjust. I promise!

I am happy to report that Jalen, now twenty-one, and Aiden, eighteen, are doing great. They learned a lot from their *Crawl Before You Ball* childhood experiences. Jalen saved over $16,000 by his twenty-first birthday, and my parents and Dave and I matched his savings, as we promised. He is now looking for his first duplex to buy. He plans on renting the other side out as an income stream and to create wealth. Sounds like his auntie, right? Aiden has started college and is learning to live on a budget. He asks constantly for access to his trust fund, and we laugh. Let me just say that Aiden is still crawling, but I know he will get there one day soon.

The Joneses Are F'ing Liars

Likes 9384

Step 2: **Ignore the Joneses**. Plain and simple, no-frills, you *must* ignore them! And now, with social media, you are inundated daily with damn fakery. It used to be that you only had to tolerate them at church, school functions, or the office. Unfortunately, we are now stuck seeing pictures of them eating out at expensive restaurants every day (but one of them uses the oven to heat their apartment), wearing the latest designer ensembles (but their kids ain't got no damn school supplies). I saw someone post their receipt from a restaurant, and the bill was $1,100 for two people, and I nearly had a heart attack. Folks have truly lost their minds. I could go on and on. Anyone trying *that* hard to impress total strangers is on some fake shit. It's going to be particularly difficult during the holiday that I call tax season, because they're going to be out of control. New TVs, cars, cell phones, iPads, clothes—the list goes on and on. Despite what you see on reality TV or read on social media, you have to resist these influences! Remember, that's the $50,000-dollar-a-year-millionaire lifestyle. Keep saying to yourself, "I am denying myself now, so I can have more later!" And remember, their public life is a façade; you needn't be jealous. It ain't real, so don't be envious of some fake, stressful way of living. It's silly. Remember, it's crawl BEFORE you ball, not crawl and limp into early death and never have any fun in your life!

If you budget for the fun, the fun will be freakin' fun! You see, if you follow the Joneses' way of life and take your behind on vacation without a pot to piss in or a window to throw it out of, how can you actually have fun? If you are constantly worried that your credit card will be declined or that a bill will auto-draft from your checking and you can't even go out to dinner, why the hell didn't you stay yo' arse at home? I mean, really? We create unnecessary drama in our own lives doing stupid(ish) things like this. And don't hit me with "Buffie, we all deserve or want to have fun occasionally, too . . . " BS. Having fun, a.k.a. balling before you crawl, will keep yo' behind broke both financially and mentally.

Again, Words Have Power

Likes 856

Step 3: **Words have power.** Remember when I mentioned that what you say every day has the power to cast a spell on your life? CB4UB is less about learning how to budget and more about learning to work on your financial mental health. To do so, you have to eliminate the following words and phrases from your vocabulary for CB4UB to work, including any similar ones. Remember, we are *out* of the self-sabotage business. Period! Our brain controls everything in our body, so let's stop setting ourselves up for failure.

The Real Curse Words and Phrases to Eliminate from Your Vocabulary

Deserve
Can afford
Need
Have no choice
It's only ... (insert a figure)
Duty

Dig out an old jar and use a black marker to write the following in big, bold print: CB4UB Swear Jar. Each time someone in your household uses any of the words or phrases listed above, they need to insert one dollar or an IOU chore into the jar. IOU chores work better than money. I love to assign cleaning up dog poop in the yard as the chore of the week. The point is you have to *stop* using these terms and phrases. They are so dangerous. If not, you can easily convince yourself into making silly financial mistakes because of these words.

Remember when I told you that I started listening to that little devilish voice inside of me that said I *deserved* to fly to London once a month to get my hair done, even though I was only twenty years old and a full-time college student? How ridiculous was that? But I rationalized the behavior because I not only *deserved* it, I also could *afford* it, and I *needed* to get my hair done anyway. And since everyone was always begging me for money, I *had no choice* but to fly first class to London for the weekend each month to get away from them, plus the fact that *it was only* X amount of dollars, and, last, it was *my duty* as a professional to look a certain way, so I had to do it. Yet another long sentence, but it's imperative to illustrate the verbal diarrhea that is our conscience, conning us into f'ing up our money goals. This is how we rationalize this type of behavior in our minds. Chile, nobody owes you anything, and you deserve nothing!

This new epidemic of entitlement will ensure that we all stay broke financially and mentally. And it's all by design. Trust me. SocieTHEY needs a working class. If we allow ourselves to be tricked into believing we should spend everything we earn to live the life that we *think* wealthy people live, we will stay broke financially and mentally. And the rich will keep getting rich off the backs of the working class.

Do you now see how this happens? Stop using those CB4UB curse words immediately! In our household, we keep the jar out year-round as a way to constantly check ourselves. If you like it, do the same. It only takes about thirty days to eliminate those words from your daily vocabulary. My hope is that you'll catch yourself beginning to say one of those words or phrases, and you'll check yo'self with empathy. Once you begin checking yourself—stopping yourself mid-sentence when you start to say one of those words or phrases—you're ready to move on to the next step in the CB4UB program.

CHAPTER 5

The Crawling Phase—Needs vs. Wants

● ●

THIS IS THE PART where folks typically get a little peeved with me. So, please prepare yourself. And know that my shadiness is done with love because I want you to have your heart's desire and peace of mind. In addition, throwing some shade has its role: it sparks a reaction and can help motivate people. I told ya, I am real.

The Big-Es are what I call absolutely unnecessary big, annual expenses. These typically occur around Valentine's Day, birthdays, anniversaries, tax season (if you are due large refunds), and worst of all, the commercialization of the Christmas holiday. You're probably rolling your eyes right now and thinking, This girl is crazy.

I hate it when people skip paying their bills in December, so they can put on airs and ball out of control during the holiday season. *It's one of the worst annual financial decisions that you can possibly make.* And trust me, more people than you realize make this same mistake year after year. Remember the definition of insanity? Doing the same thing over and over again and expecting a different outcome; well, stop it y'all. It's not worth it! Why would you want to put yourself in that stressful position in January? I know how so many of you rationalize it: "Well, I can be late on the rent or mortgage because I'll get my tax refund in January, and I'll have enough to pay for both months." Then, when your employer does not issue your W-2 until January 31, you come into my office crying and trying to scheme how to file your tax return with your last pay stub. It happens every year! Now, if you have *never* done this before, let me give you your equivalent. You charge up your credit cards on Black Friday and throughout December and cry about it later in January. Sound familiar? This is actually the norm for most Americans. If I am describing you, please don't feel bad. I repeat, this is the norm for most Americans. The most important thing is that you are actively making a change today.

Big-E Holidaze

Likes 3990

I am not saying you can't put up a tree and have a big family dinner. I am saying you don't need to go into debt to celebrate the holidays each year. When I started developing CB4UB, I didn't mention the holidays. I, for one, love Christmas. It's my favorite holiday. My sister was gracious enough to allow me to hog the Christmas holiday with her children, Jalen and Aiden. And my Aunt Dee Dee, may she rest in peace, allowed me to do the same with her son Terrence. Courtney and Dee Dee were both single parents, and though they were perfectly capable of creating their own traditions, they allowed me to create them for their kids. I will forever be grateful to them for that.

I look forward to Christmas every year. I arranged for the boys to go ice skating at the St. Regis Hotel and have a cup of cocoa and s'mores with Santa Claus. We bought the latest gadgets and spoiled those sweet little babies rotten. I decided to add holidays into the CB4UB mix when I got married and lost my flippin' mind. For some odd reason, I thought I *needed* to put up the largest tree in the neighborhood and have the best outdoor and indoor holiday décor on the street because I was a doctor's wife. That was what was expected of me.

Then there was the interracial marriage thing. I was the Black wife, so, of course, I felt like I needed to go overboard with extravagant gifts for our nieces and nephew on my husband's side of the family. My sisters-in-law—and I use that term lightly—never liked or understood me. I doubt they even tried. Lord knows that I did. Anyway, long story short, I did the most for the kids (who are all amazing) because I love them, but it was also an attempt to stave off additional looks of bewilderment and utter disdain for me. I can remember one Christmas spending over $3,000 on presents for family members. Remember, we don't even have kids. I started listening to that devilish voice inside that said, "Oh, Buffie, you HAVE it, so SPEND it!" People expect it from you. How else will they know how successful you are? I fell for it and spent a ridiculously high sum of money on holiday décor, presents, and our annual holiday party.

When the snow dust and tinsel settled, and David and I had our annual budget planning meeting, I realized then that we had lost our damn minds. See, you have to keep checking yourself at every stage in life. I remember sobbing while going through our last three months (October, November, and December) of our credit card statements, bank statements, and cash receipts. As punishment, we sat down one weekend and went through each transaction one by one. I decided then and there that my husband and I would not give each other Christmas, anniversary, birthday, or Valentine's Day gifts for a few years to test out my CB4UB plan. I hate it when people have advice for you that they haven't taken in their own lives. Don't you? I also decided that the swanky, annual Purselle holiday party was a thing of the past. No more hiring ten servers and two bartenders. No more paying through the nose for a catering service in December. I decided that we would eat and drink up someone else's hard-earned money for a few years! And as for the family, only immediate family members, i.e., nieces and nephews, would receive gifts from us, and by gifts, I mean one gift per kid with a limit of fifty dollars each. We would rather invest in their investment accounts. As for their parents, they would receive a lovely, heartwarming holiday card.

It might sound harsh, but it isn't, especially when you realize that you can reach your goals faster if you cut the

Big-Es out. And for real, though, no matter how much money I spent, the women married to my husband's brothers were never going to like me. And on my side of the family—Jalen, Aiden, and Terrence loved the tradition of being together much more than the extravagant gifts.

Teaching Your Kids to Crawl During the Holidays

♡ ◯ ▽   ◻

Likes 37894

If you have kids, Christmas and birthday Big-Es are going to be tough. This is how you handle it: give your kids one gift each at Christmas. It won't kill them. Believe me! If the kids are over the age of seven, give them a gift card or cash and let them buy what they want. I like this idea because you can track their spending and see if they save any of it. When we purchase gift cards from our bank, it allows us to track the kids' spending. We tend to add a little challenge with our nephews and nieces. We give them the option to cash in the card, meaning give it back to us, and we will save it for thirty days so they can earn an interest payment from us. This teaches them the value of delayed gratification (crawling) and making money while they sleep (balling). I can remember our Jalen saying, "So, let me get this straight. If I give you back this gift card, in thirty days you will give me more money just because I didn't spend the money on the card?" He was like, "Is this a scam?" David and I giggled and said, "Nope!" Let me tell you, that teenager got the concept of compound interest instantly, which is how he has so much in savings now as a young man. I am so proud of him. We are still working on Aiden.

When a birthday rolls around, resist the urge to throw a ridiculously expensive, super sweet six-year-old birthday party for Instagram. Instead, have a simple old-fashioned party at home. The kids will still have fun; kids don't need much. A lot of extravagant parties are about parents trying to show off for neighbors, family members, and the parents of your kid's friends. What you might not realize is that you are teaching your kids that they should place value on what others think of them. Remember, they will witness your breakdown when the devil comes to collect after all that showboating. Money sickness PTSD will plague them forever, so stop it now.

A Couple of Couple's Holidays

Likes 9040

Now, when your anniversary and Valentine's Day roll around, don't slip up! My husband prepares a romantic dinner for me (I'm not a good cook, but he is), and we watch a romantic movie at home. Now to be fair, Dave and I are a little bit anti-social. We don't like crowds so we look forward to staying home, but it can become something special for you and your loved one as well. You have to ignore the Joneses on Valentine's Day. You know, the girl in the office who receives $500 worth of flowers, balloons, edible arrangements, stuffed animals, and flaunts it all in front of the women who haven't received anything. Ignore her trifling behind! Chances are she sent all that crap to herself. And frankly, I wouldn't want a man who was so frivolous with his loot. Of course, gifts are not my love language, but no judgment if it is yours. Just take a few years off and stack your money. You can resume a pared-down version when you've reached your savings goals. Remember, it's crawl *before* you ball, not crawl and *never* ball. Keep your eyes on the prize. When you discover how much extra money you have in the bank because of the loss of the Big-Es, you won't mourn them anymore.

An Anniversary to Remember

Likes 1334

Funny story, Dave and I were in the kitchen laughing and drinking a glass of wine. My mother-in-law, the beautiful Rev. Kerry Purselle, FaceTimed us to say, "Happy Anniversary." Dave and I looked at each other confused and immediately inquired if she was OK, because it wasn't our anniversary. She laughed and made a joke about being in her seventies and us forgetting our own wedding anniversary. Dave and I looked at each other and realized that it was, in fact, our wedding anniversary. My mother-in-law said that Dave's dad would be in trouble for forgetting, and I told her I was delighted that we had both forgotten. It's a great accomplishment, but it doesn't need to be something that we go into debt for each year to show each other how much we care. I was so pleased we both forgot that I posted a video about it on social media. We explained that we have been living the CB4UB way of life for so long that even when we stopped working the steps (because we had achieved our financial goals), they stayed with us. It's become our new normal, and we are just fine with that.

Needs vs. Wants

Likes 9984

Now that you're over the loss of the Big-Es, let me state something profound. I mentioned it earlier, but you might have missed it, so here it is again: **your problem isn't with money; your problem is your ever-evolving wants**. All right, now we are ready to do some good old-fashioned math. How much do you earn per month? In other words, what is your net income after taxes, insurance, bankruptcy payments, child support, tax levies, whatever you have going on? How much deposits into your account each month? This the money that you can actually do stuff with.

Write down *all* sources of income. If you receive child support, alimony, social security, then write down how much. I ask this because when I have one-on-one appointments with new clients who want a personal CB4UB plan, most people lie for some reason. It's silly. You've hired me and spent your hard-earned money in an effort to fix your finances but choose to lie about your income? Repeatedly, folks bloat their income verbally, not realizing that I am going to ask for actual documents. It never ceases to amaze me how much people care what others think; it rules their lives and aids in the ultimate self-fulfilling prophecy of doom that affects the personal finances of so many Americans. This is how I *know* personal finance problems are not about a budget. It's not about math. It's about your financial mental health.

We need to work with actual figures when we develop your personal plan of action. Don't tell me, "The gross is this, and if I work hard and meet the quota, I'll receive a bonus." I need to know what you are guaranteed to bring home every month without all the "ifs." People in my family are the worst at this crap. Typically, folks who own seasonal and year-round businesses, in general, tend to budget based on what they *hope* to earn, not on what they *actually* earn. I can hear one of my uncles now—"If I prepare twenty-five hundred returns this year, I can buy that new Porsche," while knowing full well he prepared a thousand returns last year, so how in hell is he going to make such a big jump in one year? This is *very* dangerous thinking. It reminds me of cringing and falling out of my chair laughing when I watched George Stephanopoulos interview Donald Trump some years ago. George asked Trump what his net worth was, and Trump said that his net worth depended on how he felt that day. Gimme a break! There is a simple mathematical formula to determine net worth, and there is nowhere in that equation for feelings and emotions. Feeling like you can earn a bonus this year shouldn't be factored into the monthly income that I am asking you about. It's a trap.

Please jot down your income sources in the space provided below.

....

....

....

....

....

....

Determine Your Liabilities, Not Your Liar-abilities

Likes 9665

Just as I wanted you to be real about determining your REAL monthly income, we also need to figure out your liabilities, not your liar-abilities. People lie about their monthly expenses just like they lie about their monthly income. I guess in part because they don't want to become severely depressed by looking at how much they actually owe, not to mention the shame that we attach to our fiscal mistakes. Going through your income and expenses is an excellent way to check yourself. Remember, when Dr. Dave and I decided to get our *ish* together, we sat down and went through our last three months of bank statements, cash receipts, and credit card statements. Well, now it's your turn to do the same. It's a painful task, but it will definitely help you check your liabilities.

Let's think about your monthly expenses. List your expenses in the space provided below. And I mean *everything*. Anyone you have to write a check to on a monthly basis due to a debt, list it. Now, write down the amount you've spent on food, fuel, and emergencies. Oh, and don't forget to include the Cash Apps and Zelles that you send each month, bailing out family members and friends. No judgment. Be real. This won't work if you can't be.

Use the space below to jot down your monthly expenses. No need to be super fancy; just grab a pen or pencil and write. There are more sophisticated spreadsheets and journals for you to use at the end of the book. This task prompts you to be actionable while reading. It also helps you recall what you're learning.

We now come to the liar-ability section! Write down the expenses in the space below that you should be paying but aren't, such as student loans, child support (shame on you), credit cards (you know, the ones from college that you forgot about), and any other expenses.

....

....

....

....

Make the Cut—Determine Wants vs. Needs

Likes 1389

I love this topic. This is my favorite step. I bet you think it's easy to determine wants from needs, right? Wrong! Unfortunately, we allow our emotions and that little devilish voice deep within to coerce us into believing that wants are, in fact, needs. The devil absolutely loves misery, so he is always trying to confuse your financial mentality.

> A **want** is something you desire
> but is NOT required to have to survive.
> A **need** is something you must have in order to live.

When you think in these terms, it is easier to figure out the difference between the two. Use this black and white definition. There is no gray area between a want and a need.

> **Let's start with this easy exercise to determine wants from needs:**
> 1. Purchasing a new car when your current vehicle runs fine. **Want** or **Need**?
> 2. Getting your hair done every Friday. **Want** or **Need**?
> 3. Ordering dinner using a delivery service app. **Want** or **Need**?
> 4. Buying the kids a new gaming system. **Want** or **Need**?
> 5. Taking the family on vacation. **Want** or **Need**?

How did you do? How many needs did you come up with? I hope zero because none of those scenarios qualify as a need. Look back at the definitions. A need is something you have to have to survive—and none of those qualify! You won't die if your hair isn't fried, dyed, and laid to the side every Friday. You might look like a hot damn mess, but you will survive. We all looked a mess during the COVID-19 lockdown when barbers and hair salons were closed. What I'm saying is, you can do this for a while to help meet your financial goals. And you certainly won't die if you don't have a brand-new shiny car when your beater still cranks every morning.

Now, you may think I am evil for saying your kids don't need to go on vacation this year, but they don't! They won't perish. Do you know what will make them perish? Giving Mickey Mouse, Minnie Mouse, and Sleeping Beauty all your damn money and not being able to keep a roof over your kids' heads. Parents get themselves into so much financial trouble over this particular want—giving their children everything they couldn't do or have when they were young. It's understandable for you to want to make a good life for your kids and expose them to new things. But if you allow them to do *everything*, and you know darn well it's not in the budget, you are setting yourself and your kids up for failure. You will unknowingly teach them that it's OK to do whatever they want and figure out how to pay for it later. And that it's OK to give in to the little devilish voice within that causes money sickness. I know this is difficult. It takes time to adjust. CB4UB teaches us to be OK with that process.

What is money anyway? And why do so many of us place such a huge value on it? Money is a social construct that someone said has value, and we all believe it. It is made up of 25 percent linen and 75 percent cotton. It's no different from your wants. Think about this: If some catastrophic world event occurs and we are forced to live in a world without our usual comforts, what becomes truly valuable? Will your Gucci belt, Chanel bag, limited-edition Jordans, or exclusive golf membership help you survive? Do you think you will be able to barter with those items? Hell, no! No one will care about that shit when there is food scarcity and no running water. Those wants, and money for that matter, will become instantly worthless. Do you know what the new currency will be? **NEEDS**. Food, water, shelter, protection, and medicine. Do you know why? Because our basic needs have always been the only things that actually matter and that have real value in this world.

Homework Time!

♡ ◯ ◁   ⊓

Likes 4759

The following is a link to our CB4UB Needs vs. Wants Spreadsheet.

www.justbeingbuffie.com/budget

I would like you to take your most recent three months of bank and credit card statements, cash receipts, and anything else you have related to your finances and input the data. The spreadsheet forces you to take each transaction and categorize it as a *need* or a *want*. When you finish, you may likely see that you have money to save because it will be in the Wants column. This exercise might take a while, so it's best to start it on the weekend or when you are off from work. Most clients become emotional when going through their statements, line item by line item, but it is a necessary part of your CB4UB journey. Those modern apps that automatically download your transactions and categorize them for you aren't effective in getting you to *see* that YOU have a hand in your personal financial issues. Sometimes it is important to do things old school. Be very tactile—print out your statements, use a ruler and a highlighter—and do the work. Discuss out loud whether each transaction is a need or a want. It really will change your perspective.

CHAPTER 6

The Most Important Investment
You Will Ever Make

THE MOST COMMON QUESTION I am asked daily is, "Buffie, I have some extra money saved, and I want to get into investing. What do you recommend?" My response is the same response I have had for over twenty years—"Invest in yourself!" Obviously, this annoys some but intrigues the ones who understand what the CB4UB program is all about.

CB4UB is doing what you have to do, so you can do what you want to do later. Remember, if you do your chores and homework, you can go outside and play. So, do your damn chores and homework and make life easier! The world of investing is no different. Why would I suggest you get into cryptocurrency and the stock market when you haven't even saved two years of what it costs you to be you? If you haven't done the minimum of at least investing in yo' damn self (your chores and homework), you have no business indulging yourself or anybody else (taking yo' behind outside to play)! You *do* know that investing in stocks, cryptocurrency, and real estate is basically saying publicly that you believe in those investments, right? It's like the meme—"That's my man (insert any investment) and I'm gonna stand beside him (it)." I hope this makes sense and that I made you laugh.

The Trouble with Three to Six Months

Likes 947

Some "financial experts" recommend you save only three to six months of living expenses, but I have never agreed with that recommendation. Most "financial experts" assume the average American has other investments, such as a retirement plan, they could use if the *ish* hits the fan. Having only six months saved is like saying, "Use this amount before you tap into your REAL savings." I understand that *most* people, regardless of their socioeconomic status, live from direct deposit to Cash App, to title pawn, to direct deposit. The secret poor come from all sectors of life. As a tax practitioner, mortgage broker, and insurance agent, I've seen and heard it all. I know exactly what folks spend their money on from day to day, and it ain't a savings or retirement account. So, there will be no one to bail you out if the world comes to a screeching halt. And I have proof. Look at what happened when COVID-19 hit. The U.S. government barely gave folks a few thousand dollars to survive when the country literally shut down. The government told us to stay home, as if everyone could **afford** (dangerous word) to.

It reminds me of what happened when Hurricane Katrina hit years ago. I remember hearing folks, those who have always had a good job, a loving family, and substantial savings to use in a crisis, have the audacity to say, "Why didn't they just leave when the government told them to leave?" I recall getting into long, drawn-out discussions that turned into arguments with these folks when their comments revealed how freaking out of touch and unempathetic they were. I even lost a few friends. If you barely get by from day to day, *how* can you go anywhere? Who would provide gas for the car (if you were lucky enough to have a car)? Who would supply the bus fare, food for evacuation, and lastly, where the hell would you go? Many barely had enough money to live, and even if they were able to leave the state, who was going to pay for the hotel when they reached their next destination? Not the government, I can tell you that, not anyone.

Not everyone has a family or feels comfortable enough to stay with their extended family when in crisis. Having family that you can rely on is a form of generational wealth and privilege. This is why investing in yourself is so important. It also provides you with the most wonderful feeling in the entire world. It's called PEACE of MIND. The peace of mind in knowing that if something awful happens, you have money to take care of yourself. That's the goal:

Earn ➡ Save ➡ Ball Occasionally ➡ Repeat

When you do ball occasionally, ball out with the interest earned from the savings and NEVER EVER touch your savings. That is how the rich stay rich. They live off the interest earned from their wealth and never touch the principal balance. And now, so will you.

Why I Don't Really F with Banks

I can remember as a child walking over to my Big Daddy's house to help feed the chickens and play with the biddies (baby chicks). If you aren't Southern and familiar with the term Big Daddy, please allow me to enlighten you. Big Daddy is a term of endearment and respect for an elderly male in the family. My Big Daddy was my grandmother's uncle. I was very close to him. He was born in 1899 and couldn't read or write but was as clever as the day is long.

Math was his thing. While helping my Big Daddy care for those chickens and biddies, I learned about hiding money in the chicken coop. My Big Daddy didn't fully trust the banks, and during his lifetime he damn well shouldn't have trusted them. He didn't believe in keeping all his eggs in one basket. He kept some money in the bank, some invested in land, and the rest he hid in the chicken coop. I think that the modern-day equivalent to the chicken coop is blockchain and cryptocurrency. It's locked up, and hopefully, if invested wisely, no one can take it from you. And there is no barrier to entry for people of color yet.

I remember posting about not understanding why so many young people spent so much of their hard-earned money on jewelry. One of my social media followers commented, which changed my entire perspective. She wrote that Black people have a history of having their money and land stolen from them. Many people still live with that generational monetary trauma of actually doing what you are supposed to do, only to have it taken away. She went on to say that jewelry, clothes, and cars are portable, meaning they are things that you can easily take with you if someone tries to steal them from you. They are things that could be used to barter or sell if you needed to do so. I cried when I read that. It hit me like a ton of bricks. She was right. I had to check my privilege and remember whence we ALL came. My version of distrust for traditional banks (i.e., buying jewelry and expensive cars) is investing in real estate. So, I knew there was some generational trauma healing that needed to take place for us all.

When you deposit money into a bank account, it is considered an investment. That's one of the reasons why I keep very little money in my checking account. Banks typically pay diddly-squat for checking accounts, so why would you keep the bulk of your money there? I know, I know, we have all been taught to keep our money in the bank. We need to discuss what bank, not the bank that has your checking account. Be disciplined with your payroll and split the deposit. If you know you'll need half of your payroll for bills and the other half can be saved, set it up as a direct deposit.

Do *not* link your checking and savings accounts! This is my pet peeve. You basically are just setting up two checking accounts. The banks will lure you in with "overdraft protection," but all they are doing is moving money from your "savings" to your checking account and charging yo' crazy arse a fee for the service. I swear banks are the ultimate con game. They make the public think that they make money by charging you fees, but the fees are chump change. They really make their money by investing *your* deposits and giving you nothing for it. Yes, you read that correctly. Banks make their money by investing your deposits and giving you very little in return. They don't even guarantee you a loan for your car, home, or even a damn credit card, but they take your money and lend it out to others and make billions of dollars doing it. It's all legal, too. Back in the day, banking was about relationships. If you deposit your money here, we will be there for you when you need to buy a car, send your kid to college, take care of a loved one, or buy a home. Sadly, this is no longer the case. The most trusted bank in the world was once Wells Fargo Bank. After we all learned that the bank's staff was pressured into opening new accounts without the consent of the actual banking client, we should have known then that it was time to hold banks accountable.

So, if you shouldn't keep the bulk of your money in your checking account, where should you keep it? In a high-yield savings account that is separate from your checking account, because you need to get something out of your investment. Savings should be with an institution (not necessarily a traditional bank, but they should be FDIC insured and offer a high-yield account). High yield means that they pay you some damn money for your investment. High yield is typically 0.40 percent APR (annual percentage rate) or higher. Some high-yield savings accounts have stipulations on when you can draw on your money, so it is important for you to check with the institution. Why should you choose a different institution other than your checking account bank? Because you need to eliminate the ease of transfer. Your savings should be somewhere secure, where it is virtually impossible for you to easily get your money out. You have to trick yourself into forgetting about your savings account, so compound interest can do its thang. Think of your savings account like the movie *Gremlins*. Feed them plenty of water, food, and sunlight after midnight, and forget about them. They will multiply and grow your money like crazy. If you didn't get the *Gremlins* reference, it's a movie from 1984, and I highly recommend it.

Devil Card and Credit Cards

Likes 2323

Debit cards are the devil, and I rebuke them. I can picture it now—a smoky room filled with greedy bankers plotting their next scheme. Let's create a card that gives the illusion of a credit card, but it's actually tied to our customer's bank accounts. We can *allow* them to overdraft the account using the card as we *allow* them to do with checks and charge them a fee for it. And we can make them think that we are doing this as a value-added service. Well, what happens if the card is stolen or there is a data breach? Let's freeze the customer's money and investigate the fraud with no guarantee of replacing it. Brilliant! And voilà, the devil card, a.k.a. the debit card, was born out of the fiery pits of hell.

When debit cards first came out, I was like, "Oh, hell no." I knew exactly what these shady arse bankers were up to with this scam masquerading as a service. They were preying on the average American's need to *feel* like they have a shiny plastic credit card without providing any of the benefits of a shiny plastic credit card. There is that word again—*feeling*. Marketing is all about feelings. We are humans, and our feelings are valid. We just need to make sure that our feelings are ours and not a projection from the media. Remember, we talked about focusing on what YOU want, not what SocieTHEY tells you that you want through deceptive marketing tactics.

I told you financial literacy is less about a budget and more about your mental health. Anyway, back to my total and utter disdain for the ruse that is the devil card. I remember my clients having the most overdrawn accounts that I had ever seen in my twenty-plus years of working in the accounting field, largely due to the almighty devil card. If folks had trouble managing a damn checkbook, just imagine the havoc that one bank account and two debit cards inflicted on the average American's household finances. I routinely told my clients to cut up their debit cards and not use them. If they couldn't explain the benefit of using the card, then it was time to destroy it.

At least with checks, folks would check with each other (pun intended) before writing one. With devil cards, I think your brain is subliminally tricked into thinking that you have a Black American Express with no limit because folks are out there swiping away with negative bank balances and closed checking accounts. And traditional banks will happily allow you to swipe your life away. Then they decided to try to steal your savings accounts by marketing the nifty tool of linking your savings account to your checking account to ensure that you never have overdraft fees again. What a damn lie! Like I mentioned before, if you use your savings to bail out your checking, then you have two checking accounts. Savings are meant to be saved. Etch the following into your brain: *we use the interest generated from the savings account and NEVER touch the principal balance.* That's how the rich stay rich.

The Truth About Credit Cards

♡ ♡ ▽   ⊓

Likes 940

They are the best damn thing since sliced bread. They really are. Folks love to say stay away from credit cards out of fear they'll jack up your finances and credit. No, they won't. Practice your financial meditation and try to block out the financial PTSD flashbacks from college and your childhood.

You are an adult now and know better. Stop punishing yourself and stifling your financial growth for prior money and credit mistakes. Remember what I said, you will never progress if you stay in a constant state of blame. If used properly, credit cards are an extremely useful tool to help you grow your wealth.

Ain't nothing like using someone else's money for your daily and large purchases. It's the best and is financially savvy. Let me explain. If you obtain a credit card and use it the same way you were using that damn devil card for your everyday needs (within reason) and pay it off in full each month (like you would have done with the devil card), you will build credit, earn credit card points, and protect your real money from fraud. Let me break this down a little more. When you use your devil card daily, the bank automatically withdraws the amount swiped from your checking account. When you use a credit card, there is no automatic deduction. This is the part that gets some folks into trouble. The way to resolve this is after you use your credit card, go home and transfer the money from your checking account to pay it off. Do this until you feel that you are disciplined enough to make one payment before the end of each month. You may think, "Well, then why not just use the darn devil card?" Well, the devil card doesn't provide you with the same benefits that the credit card does. When you master using credit wisely, you won't have to deplete your cash immediately. You can leverage your debt by using fabulous offers like 0 percent APR for twelve months, also known as no interest charges as long as you pay the balance off within twelve months.

Remember earlier how we discussed the bank giving you that shiny, plastic ruse of a devil card, and when there is a data breach, they tell you that you're basically on your own until they've investigated? Well, your credit card company won't do that. They have your back. They will immediately put the money back on your card and investigate *without* causing you any financial strain. You wanna know why? Because it's *their* money. With the bank, they don't give an F because it's *your* money. Get it? Clearly, I can't stand the banks based on what I told you earlier, but do your research. If the bank isn't offering anything for the investment of your money, find one that will.

Free Ain't Free

Likes 3434

Stop giving folks your personal information, PLEASE! Why does every Tom, Dick, and Andy Cohen need your Social Security number, life story, and blood type? They don't. I love going to a new dentist or doctor, and their paperwork requests not only my health insurance card and number but also my Social Security number. Make it make sense. If you have my insurance card, why the hell do you need a Social Security number? I don't care if you have a -125 credit score. Stop giving folks your Social Security number unless there is a real need to do so.

You have probably figured out that these new, rather inexpensive tech gadgets that were made to "make our lives better" are spying on us. Yep. The money is *not* made on that TV purchase. It's made by selling the data that they collect while we use them. I can't tell you how many companies used to contact me daily requesting that I sell my tax practices' client data, not their Social Security numbers, but how much they make, where they live, how many kids they have, and so on and so forth. Information is the real currency today. Knowing as much about their potential client as possible helps companies in the pursuit of helping us part with our hard-earned money. Do I have smart TVs, Alexa, Ring doorbell, social media, and an iPhone? Yep, just like everyone else. At this point, it's pretty unavoidable unless you live off the grid. And trust me, I am diligently working on a plan to do just that. I am not saying you shouldn't enjoy technology. I am saying be cognizant of the fact that when someone says something is free, it usually means that *you* are the product because free ain't free.

CHAPTER 7

The Investment of Generational Wealth

· ·

I HOSTED A LIVE YouTube session with someone I follow on TikTok who has since become a close friend. Her name is Patrice E. Jones. She is also one of my book's editors.

Anyway, back to the YouTube show. Patrice was a guest on my *justbeingBuffie* YouTube show to discuss the topic of generational wealth. Patrice is the steward of over one hundred acres of land left to her family by her great-great-grandmother. She taught me during her interview that no one actually owns the land, and that is why she doesn't say she is a landowner. I have forever changed my vernacular to use land steward when discussing our properties. She gave my subscribers and me many financial gems about generational wealth, and for that I will always be grateful. It is important for people to see people who look like them, who sound like them, doing the things that we say you should be doing.

Patrice said many profound things that day, but the one that stood out to me the most—and she will likely be surprised when she reads this and edits this chapter—was when she mentioned that knowing she had the family land had enabled her to take risks in her life that she would not ordinarily take. That truly resonated with me. It shook me out of my complacency because I, too, was blessed with financial confidence, a mentality that comes from having generational wealth, only I didn't even realize it until she said that. How many of you have also been blessed with some form of generational wealth yet are unaware? We often think of generational wealth as mansions, trust funds, expensive family heirlooms, etc. She mentioned that even if she had to pitch a tent on the land, it was there for her if she needed it. Being a steward of that land probably enabled her to take a job because it was interesting and fulfilling to her—and not solely based on compensation. Being the steward of that land likely enabled her to choose love over financial stability when choosing a life partner. It allowed her to shut down that devilish voice in the back of her head. I could go on and on. Her statement is a testimony to the power of having a financial mentality. When we discuss generational wealth, folks tend to think only of billionaires, but most of us have generational wealth and just don't realize it.

How many of us have a grandparent, parent, auntie, uncle, or someone in the family who owns a home? And though we may not like where the home is or the current condition of the home, it still exists. Like Patrice said, if you truly hit rock bottom, you know you can always go to this home, even if you have to pitch a tent in the backyard. Having somewhere to live, which is one of the most important

NEEDS, *is* generational wealth. Like my grandmother says, "They ain't making any more land, so you better acquire and keep as much of it as you can." That is exactly what she did.

A Bit About My Family's Investment in Generational Wealth

Likes 5565

My childhood was spent abroad. From the ages of three to thirteen, we lived in Germany. My mother insisted that each summer my sister and I fly home to the States, to be with our family in South Georgia. My sister, Courtney, and I enjoyed a wonderfully magical childhood filled with visiting castles and other countries on weekends, but we loved coming home to Grammy's the most. We started flying by ourselves when I was six years old. Of course, my mom paid a little extra for the flight attendants to watch over us on those ten-hour flights, but I am still proud we did those trips. I remember filling out customs forms and carrying our passports and money in a pouch around our necks and under our shirts. My younger sister would stay wide awake for the entire flight—those poor flight attendants! I remember when we landed in Atlanta and met up with our uncle or aunt, who were tasked with picking us up, and the first place my sister and I begged to go to was Kentucky Fried Chicken. And we loved it. They had KFC abroad, but it tasted funny.

My grandparents were sharecroppers in South Georgia. They had ten children; you know, back then, if you had a farm, you needed to have children to help work the land. And boy, did they! My grandmother always regales us with the tale of her giving birth to my Aunt Phyllis in the cotton field, and then immediately going back to finish her shift in the fields. She was trying to teach us about having a strong work ethic in a rather dramatic way. My grandmother is multi-talented and gifted, but I must say that she is most gifted mathematically. She passed that skill on to her kids and grandkids. She was so good that she kept the books for the land steward, Mr. L. When my grandparents' kids were old enough to help my grandfather work the fields, my grandmother got a job. She started saving the money from her job to get her family out of the sharecropping situation, because she understood math and knew that it was a very bad deal. She worked hard, bought some land, and had a small home built for her growing family. They got out of the sharecropping deal and began growing crops on their own land for which they were stewards.

The security of having that land gave my grandmother the financial mentality to start a business and grow her family's wealth. She decided to invest in single-wide trailers in the seventies and rented them out on some of their properties. My grandmother also had another house built on the land for our extended family to use. Big Daddy and Big Mamma lived in that home.

My grandmother continued investing in a small lot here and there over the years, all paid for in full. See, when you change your financial mentality and start living in your new normal, you can do and achieve anything that you set your mind to do. My mom and her siblings didn't have the finest clothes, but they had the first home in town with two bathrooms. They may not have been able to take extravagant vacations, but the sacrifices their parents made then enabled their children to do so. And though my grandmother amassed property and her children were successful, she lived in the same house that she had built all those years ago until she moved in with my mom and dad. That's something else I want to leave you with. When you start to notice that you have significant savings and investments and move up in your position and financial salary at work, please don't be so quick to move to a bigger and better home. That's also a trick. Just because your finances change doesn't mean you need to change the way you live. That's what happens to your new wealth when you try to show it off: you spend it. Remember, it's all about your financial mentality.

Some people might have thought putting single-wide trailers on your land next to your family home was tacky, but my grandmother didn't factor in what others thought into the equation. She did what made financial sense. Remember the example I mentioned earlier of Trump and his net worth? Emotions and feelings have no value in math. She took the risk and bought those trailers, rented them out, and saved every red cent for her kids and grandkids. She created a safe community for church members and for people who looked like her, all while earning passive income. And anyone who helped in the fields on my grandparents' land could have whatever they harvested.

I remember having to shell, blanch, and freeze peas for my grandmother's tenants, people at our church, and anyone else who needed food. At the time, my cousins and I hated it. We moaned and groaned because it was hard work, and we would rather be flirting with boys and skating at the Skate Palace, but now that we are adults with busy lives and families of our own and look back on those times, we only remember giggling and the fun we had together as cousins. We remember how happy everyone was to see us when we came around to deliver our care packages with our grandmother, and how she beamed with pride when she bragged about how we practically did everything ourselves. We didn't realize it then, but Grammy was also teaching us about the value of giving back, a responsibility that comes with having generational wealth.

For all the people whom she blessed, knowing Mrs. Dot and her granddaughters would be delivering food helped them take risks, because food was one less thing they had to worry about. This is an excellent example of how helping people can be a good thing. It's not enabling as in the case we discussed before. The reason this helped instead of enabled is that they had a vested interest in the process. By helping to harvest the food, it felt less like a handout to have someone shell, blanch, and freeze the food for you. People take pride in a hard day's work. I am actually crying right now as I write this because my family no longer maintains Grammy's garden. As land stewards, I recently bought a greenhouse and carved out some space on our land to grow food. I look forward to our nephews and my young cousins helping us shell, blanch, and freeze bags of fresh veggies to give to our loved ones, employees, tenants, and anyone in need. I plan to carry on Grammy's legacy and her version of generational wealth. And by doing so, the next generation of our family will hopefully do the same.

The Investment of Family

Likes 5356

Most families no longer embrace the family lifestyle of living together, working together, thriving together, and working toward the same goal(s). My heart breaks for the connectedness we have lost as a people, my family included. Why do you think social media is so popular? Humans crave connection with other humans. There is something about living together on the same land, in proximity, so you can't ignore each other, that brings a family together and forces everyone to recall those old values from our ancestors. It is in our DNA. Remember back in the day, everyone, regardless of their race, lived on family land. The disconnect of living far away from each other is yet another reason we suffer financially, not because we can't physically walk next door to ask for a handout, but because we are not next door to help prevent us from creating the situation that forced us to need a handout in the first place.

Why can't we get back to families living together, thriving together, and working together toward a common goal? I brought this topic up on my show once, and my subscribers told me that it works in theory but just can't happen. I disagreed because, as I stated earlier, I am not someone who gives advice that I have not taken in my own life. My nephew and several of my cousins have lived with us over the years. When they moved to Atlanta for college or to start their lives, I wanted to make sure that rent was the last thing they worried about. They were given jobs at my office or my husband's office, and we helped them with a plan to make it on their own. They didn't have to leave until they met the goals that we set forth with them.

So back to the YouTube show, I had a subscriber call in who argued with me for five minutes with all the usual reasons about why a family lifestyle can't work anymore. She said, "Everyone doesn't get along with their family, to which I responded, "You have a valid point." She said she has tried to help before, and her family members "tore up her house and ran up her bills." I told her that I was sorry to hear that. She said she "needed her personal space." I said that I totally understood that want. And she added, "No, I *need* my personal space." I then told her that personal space is a luxury that we have convinced ourselves is a need but is, in fact, a *want*. If our ancestors could live in a one-room shack, sleep on the floor with ten other people next to a wood-burning fireplace, I think we can survive living in a home with other people. She said I was extreme. I disagreed with her. As I have mentioned before, we allow deceptive marketing tricks and societal pressures to dictate how we see the world.

The media depicts successful people living in a single-family dwelling with only their immediate family and their dog, and if our way of life differs in any way, we believe that we have somehow failed. We have to stop allowing that devilish voice in the back of our heads to dictate our life choices. Who the hell (pun intended) cares what some marketing firm, who likely hired a focus group of lost souls, deems what success in America should look like? Why should that rule your life's choices? So many people from other countries come to the U.S. and fight diligently to ensure that their culture stays within the family. They urge family members not to assimilate too much into American society, so much so that they live together. Do you think they all get along? Do you think some of them need their personal space? Yes, but the ultimate goal of making sure that everybody makes it, in *their* view, is all that matters.

So, let's revisit the question again: Why can't families live together? Why is it so important to kick your kid(s) out of the house when they turn eighteen? Who made up that stupid rule? If you think about it, it is potentially one of the single best ways to set them up for financial failure. How are you gonna kick your kid out when they have depended on you for eighteen years? Of course, it doesn't work. Do they call you to help make rent every other month? Absolutely, because who taught them how to budget? And even with a budget, the system is set up for them to fail because rents are so ridiculously high. Doesn't it make more sense for them to live at home? If you want to teach them responsibility, give them a bill to pay. Draw up a rental contract and charge them rent equivalent to the cable TV or power bill and save the damn money for them. Or, use it if you need it.

Why are we in such a hurry to have a whole bunch of empty rooms in the house? Remember how I moved my cousin in when I bought my first house? If someone in the family has a house big enough and needs help making the mortgage each month, I am a big proponent of moving folks in. Hell, even move in the ones who don't have a job. Their new job would be cleaning the damn house and taking care of the kids. Give them the job title of house manager. That will enable you to have some free time and save money on childcare costs. Their behind would be a chef, house cleaner, day-care worker, and whatever else you can come up with for room and board. And I would draw that up in a work agreement. And if no one owns a home, but everyone has high rents, I suggest renting one large home and move everybody in (if the landlord is good with it). Then split the bills and save some money. We have to get back to this, y'all. I promise you this is the answer. Is it uncomfortable? Hell yes! Will it work if everyone tries? Hell yes!

CHAPTER 8
Discover Your New Normal

- -

"WEALTH WHISPERS AND MONEY JINGLES, jangles, and screams." If you watched *That Show* or follow me on social media, you may recall this was one of my most popular quotes. I said this when two of those broads got into an argument after one of them bragged about her new home. I didn't have a problem with the person who was talking about her new home; you should allow your friends to share their failures and successes with you in life. My problem was when they started listing and comparing their assets to one another. Many people thought I was shading them because they're both nouveau riche—you know, new Bravo money—but, really, I was thinking about my way of life, crawl before you ball. I sat there while they both went on and on about their possessions all while knowing that I potentially had far more, yet kept my mouth shut, rolled my eyes, and watched the show of "showing." *Crawl Before You Ball* teaches us that when we are truly in control of our monetary mental health, we don't feel the need to show. You control money. Money doesn't control you.

As you may have already gleaned, I dedicated very little time in this book to the typical personal finance rhetoric. Perhaps you've been reading Suze "Hey, girlfriend" Orman and Dave "You can't have any debt or even a coffee *ever* in your entire life" Ramsey for years. And, guess what? When doing things their way, many of you are in the same situation you were in before you invested your money and most valuable resource, your time, and that's OK. I applaud your efforts. You took a leap of faith in an attempt to change your relationship with money. *Crawl Before You Ball* has taught you that things take time. Changing your relationship with money takes time. And while I disagree with some of Suze and Dave's beliefs, the core of what they teach is just basic personal finance. And, as I have stated over and over again, I don't believe most people's problems with money stem from a lack of budgeting. It isn't about the math. It's about your monetary mental health.

Now that you have read this damn book, it's time to do the work! You have to put what you've learned into practice in your daily life. You must start practicing everything from making your declaration of #whathadhappenedwas, to ending the cycle of codependent poverty that plagues so many of us, to checking yo'self with empathy, to crawling and blocking out the Joneses, to investing in yourself and your family. Psychologists say we can change most behaviors if we stick to it for thirty days. So, you will now begin your 30-day monetary mental health detox. Included in the supplemental chapter of this book is a 30-Day Financial Detox Journal. Use it to describe how you are feeling and how the detox is going. It's also an excellent place to vent. Additionally, I included financial worksheets for your use to work on what you learned in the Needs vs. Wants chapter of the book.

A Whole New Way Of Life

Likes 3445

CB4UB is a way of life. You have to commit to it 100 percent in order for it to work. It's hard, and only people who truly want financial freedom can excel at it. CB4UB is all about self-sacrifice—denying yourself things today so you can have more tomorrow.

I want to coin the phrase "I'm crawling, are you?" I want it to be chic and fashionable. We need to make it cool for people to save today, so they can have things later. I swear instagramification will be the death of society. Folks think that because they simply wake up and do the bare minimum, they somehow **deserve** something. It's considered not cool to sacrifice. You work hard; you should have all your heart's desires now. NOT! That's a quick way to stay broke financially and mentally. As you move forward, I ask that you practice reflection. Always try to understand how you got to where you are, so that it does not happen again. The most important reason is so you can teach your kids not to make the same mistakes. We must stop passing down this cycle of generational poverty of paycheck, to payday loan, to paycheck living.

Remember, I truly believe we create our own reality. It's difficult to commit to multiple realities, however, so choose the one that is in your best interest. You know, like those folks who are living paycheck to paycheck we discussed earlier on? They are so busy living two lives—one, projecting extreme wealth and what SocieTHEY depicts as success, and another of financial disarray and poverty. Don't be like them. Maintaining any façade is draining, and you are bound to slip up one day because the truth always comes out. Choosing a positive, uplifting reality is your best bet. If you believe in yourself, you can make a permanent change in your relationship with money. I promise you that if you put the *Crawl Before You Ball* way of life into practice, it will become your *new normal*. It won't be such a cumbersome process, and you will easily begin achieving your financial goals. It really is that simple. As I have said before, it was never solely about a damn budget. Don't listen to that BS. No smoke and mirrors. You have this. You *can* and *will* do this! I believe in you.

I am so very proud and honored that you decided to take this journey with me. I can't wait for you to do your homework and share some of it on social media. Tag me so I can follow you back and see your journey. I hope that you will come back to this book over and over again to help you during this process.

I am leaving you with the speech that I have given my clients for well over twenty years. After reading CB4UB, I hope it resonates with you:

There are NO boundaries. Say this whenever that little devilish voice starts whispering negativity in your ear, and you think you can't achieve your financial goals or anything else in your life for that matter. There are NO boundaries. They don't exist. That's the catch. That's it, for real. That is the dirty little secret no one tells you. Boundaries are created by others through ads, by some of our teachers, people in our family, faux friends, and SocieTHEY. We internalize these boundaries as facts. When you hear something or see something over and over again, even if your gut tells you that it is dead wrong, most of us internalize it as fact. In the story I shared with you about the women from *That Show* gaslighting my pain from having had multiple miscarriages, I heard them say it to me often enough that I actually started to believe it.

Another good example is how we hear a new song and dislike it, but because they keep playing it on the radio, it suddenly becomes your jam. It's just familiar, that's all. Boundaries are fake. SocieTHEY created these imaginary walls to keep us all in check, to keep us on a low vibration, financially anxious and depressed. Because if we are in that state, what will most of us do to feel better? We become reactionary and do whatever it takes to get a boost of dopamine, which means buying or eating something we shouldn't. And who loves that? Companies trying to get you to part with your coins. It's all a racket. Everything is set up to keep you in a constant state of I *want* whilst causing you to ignore your very real *needs*. Do you know why? Because your *needs* can likely be met rather easily, as you discovered when you worked on your budget. Our ever-changing and evolving wants are the problem. And the sooner you realize this the faster you will attain what it is that *you* want in this life. Do you recall how we discussed the importance of determining what you want? Concentrate on that and that alone. Don't allow anyone else to do this for you. So many of us allow SocieTHEY to make this decision for us each day, and we don't even realize it.

When Dr. Dave and I finally made the decision to stop trying to have our own biological children, we took a good look at our lives and realized that we have been blessed with children since we became a couple. Terrence, Jalen, Aiden, LesLee, Christina, Kamari, Chris, Josh, Cynthia, Ronin, Ryli, LaGhia, Job, Jonah, Louie, and Prada have all been our children. Not in the traditional sense, but who decides what a family should look like? Have my husband and I missed out on first steps, first words, basketball, lacrosse, football, plays, ballet recitals, holidays, or any of the other moments that people with children have? Nope. We have not. We created our own reality. And the reality is that we are a loving couple who have been blessed with beautiful and empathetic children who were born to us out of what a family is to us, not what SocieTHEY says a family should look like. For that, we are thankful.

This applies to your life as well. Your reality is yours and yours alone. You get to dictate what that reality is. That should be exciting and provide you with a sense of power. If fulfillment to you means acquiring land, purchasing a double-wide trailer, and driving a luxury vehicle so you can stop trading all your time for money, then do you, Boo. I salute you! So, now that you have begun your homework, please use the next thirty days to complete the journal. When you're done, I promise you that when you finally have the time to go out and play, you will find the world is your playground. *Crawl Before You Ball*.

30-DAY FINANCIAL DETOX JOURNAL

BY BUFFIE PURSELLE

THIS JOURNAL BELONGS TO:

....

....

Crawl
Before You
Ball

30-DAY DETOX

AS YOU KNOW BY NOW, my approach to financial literacy focuses more on your financial mental health and less on math and budgeting. The typical financial literacy expert preaches the same old same old—*earn more, spend less*. Well, that approach may work for some but not for everyone. Many reasons can drive chronic financial woes, but I believe generational curses of financial trauma affect many of you. For example, perhaps you grew up witnessing your parents struggle financially with the anxiety and stress of living paycheck to paycheck. Or, you were taught to take care of everyone in the family, even if it caused you financial strain. And then when you finally had a few extra dollars to yourself, you spent the money instead of saving it because it made you feel better. My hope is that CB4UB arms you with the tools you need to make positive, enduring changes to your financial mental health. Use this book as your guide to return to whenever you need it in your life.

To start, we must first deal with your financial mental health BEFORE we can tackle a budget.

"Start where you are. Use what you have.
Do what you can."
—Arthur Ashe

One reason it has taken me so long to publish this book is because I don't believe that simply reading a book will help you permanently change your relationship with money. I told you in the beginning that I get real. This process requires you to do the same. Yes, read the book but do the work of implementing CB4UB into your life. Experts claim that it takes thirty days to change a bad habit. When I created CB4UB years ago, David and I followed the 30-day detox program. I won't lie to you, it *was* difficult in the beginning. When that little devilish voice started to whisper in my ear that I needed or deserved something, I acknowledged its presence and said, "Get thee behind me, Satan." (I love a good biblical reference.) This is what Jesus said to the devil when he tried to tempt him. It's brilliant because you acknowledge the temptation and refuse to give in to it all at the same time. It's important for us to recognize our temptations, instead of pretending they don't exist. Throughout this process, it is important to treat yourself with kindness and empathy. Remember we are ALL flawed, beautiful, imperfect beings, and that is OK. And now that you are almost finished reading the book, it's time to do the work!

You will need to take the next thirty days to implement CB4UB in your life in a meaningful way. To help you do so, I have a few homework assignments for you to complete during your 30-Day Detox. I encourage you to use the space provided in this book and to post your journey on social media using the hashtag #cb4ub30daydetox and tag me for reposting. It is important to state on the public forum that you are part of CB4UB. This act helps hold you accountable and puts others on notice that you are not conducting business as usual. In six months or a year, I will continue to give away big surprises to those of you who put in the work and document your journey.

1. Acknowledge, a.k.a. #whathadhappenedwas

A rationalization means to come up with facts to defend the indefensible. The moment you stop making rationalizations and admit that you have a problem with managing your personal finances is the moment you can start to make permanent change. In the space below, take a moment to acknowledge that you have a problem with money or make a video of yourself sharing your story. Add any necessary dates and be specific about the details. For example, if you've filed bankruptcy, please include the date and details leading up to it. Or, if you're consistently overdrawn on your bank account, please list that as well. Later, once you've completed your 30-Day Detox, I suggest you revisit this assignment so you can see what space you were in when you began and where you are when you finish. Celebrating your wins is a necessary part of the program.

#whathadhappenedwas
is the MOST important homework assignment.

So, take your time! If you want to do a video, it need not be fancy. I prefer you film it with your phone because you won't lie to yourself. Many of my students in the digital course have found this assignment to be the most challenging. Some cry while filming, but it is a necessary part of your financial journey. Be honest with yourself. If you aren't honest, this process won't work.

Take this assignment seriously and don't rush!

....

....

....

....

2. Isolate the Problem

When we rationalize our bad financial habits, we often see them as an inevitable outcome of our own circumstances. If you isolate the problem that requires change, you will better equip yourself with a chance for success. Instead of pretending that financial traumas and financial PTSD don't exist, I'd like you to address them straight on.

As I've mentioned throughout, financial trauma is REAL! It is characterized as a dysfunctional reaction to chronic financial stress. Symptoms often present similarly to those who experience post-traumatic stress disorder (PTSD). Leading financial trauma expert Dr. G. Buckwalter reports that 20 percent of the population meets the criteria for financial PTSD. I believe that number is much higher. Many are unaware they're suffering from undiagnosed financial PTSD.

To consistently not have enough money is a different kind of stress—I call it SKRE$$. It keeps our physiology amped up pretty much 24/7. There is no reprieve, as we're always wired from the SKRE$$.Without the chance to recuperate, all the hormones that we need when we are truly threatened stay turned on and start chipping away at our bodies. That's why worry and SKRE$$ leave us tired and haggard looking. This is called allostatic load: the wear and tear of chronic stress beating up the systems that are weakest in any given person. So long-term financial stress can well end up as diabetes in one person, heart disease in another, and psychiatric problems in someone else.

In the space below, please discuss the financial traumas in your life and how you can make a change for the better. As you begin journaling, it may seem like you are repeating the same scenarios over and over again. That may be true. Remember, this process involves retraining your brain, which is why repetition is so important. Again, the homework assignments are designed to be a meaningful part of your CB4UB journey. For the program to work, you must complete the exercises. Please be real and honest with yourself. And remember, meaningful change takes time. That's OK.

....

....

....

3. Have Empathy for Yourself!

What do you want? Not what SocieTHEY
says that you should want.

Take some time to think deeply about this question. Please block out all the societal pressures and programmed norms. What do *you* want for yourself and your family? Are your goals based on your desires and not on what everyone else says? When you embark on the CB4UB journey, this exercise will help you come from a place of power. It's *all* about you.

STEP 01

Acknowledge what you want in life. It may feel foreign to block out what your mom, friends, and coworkers have said about what you should want in life. But it's a very liberating exercise to put yourself first.

I would like to share a quick story about a student. Dr. Dave and I hosted Zooms with our beta group of students. One evening, we discussed this particular homework assignment, and I was shocked by how many of our students had difficulties sharing what *they* wanted. When one of them began to read her assignment, I noticed that even though she said she wanted certain things, each one was really for someone else. She wanted to have more money, so that she could buy her kids what they needed. She wanted to purchase a bigger home, so she could move her mom in and help take care of her. And though the things listed were in fact her wishes—and very noble ones I might add—not one of them was singularly for her. When she finished talking, I asked, "Now, what do *you* want?" She burst into tears. And so did the other two hundred people on our Zoom call. She said she'd never thought about what she wanted for herself. She felt that it was selfish to do such a thing. I told her that that was the little devilish voice in the back of her head, and when it came to something meaningful to her, he unleashed shame. Shame for wanting something for herself that would make her life better. Now, that little voice often urges you to obtain things that you don't need, but when you begin doing the real work on yourself and attempt to heal prior traumas, shame is the number one plan in his arsenal. For this exercise, you need only acknowledge the feeling of shame for thinking about what you want in life, and then tell the devil to get behind thee, and keep moving forward.

STEP
02

Jot down your goals in the space provided below. When I am reading a book, I like to keep it on my person as I do with a cell phone. So consider keeping it within hand's reach, so you can add things here and there as you think about them.

Film a video of yourself on your mobile device discussing your financial goals for you and your family. The video should not exceed 3 minutes.

4. Get Your Immediate Family On Board

Whether you are married or shacking up and sharing bills or single, this is a crucial step in the CB4UB journey. Have a come-to-Jesus moment with your immediate family—this includes anyone who lives under your roof that you part with your money on a regular basis. Come-to-Jesus is a Southern saying similar to an intervention. Let them know that you're embarking on the CB4UB plan and what it means. For example, if you have children, have a family discussion and tell them that the family will be cutting back on its spending for a while. Explain why. It could be because you would like to purchase a family home, send the kids to private school, or take a family vacation. If you are single, have this discussion with yourself. It is important to hold yourself accountable.

Please film or record an audio of you and your family members accepting the #cb4ub challenge! Dave, Louie, Prada, and nephew son Aiden (who is in our pockets), did this as well. It is an accountability exercise and will help you when they inevitably ask you to falter. Show them the video or play the recording. It helps. Trust me.

5. Create a #cb4ub Curse Word Jar

This can be an actual jar, or if you're fancy and can come up with a tech equivalent, go for it. You get the point. Everyone who weighs in on financial decisions (including kids, who can pay with chores) must participate. Do you remember the CB4UB curse words? These are words you want to eliminate from your vocabulary. So, if you or a family member are caught using these words, add money, a chore written on paper, or whatever penalty is agreed upon, to the jar. This encourages everyone in your household to rid these words from their daily vernacular:

Deserve

Can Afford

Need

Have No Choice

It's Only (insert a figure)

Duty

6. Check Yo'self

Remember, this program is all about accountability. Don't allow outside forces or pressures to change those definitions. Stick to the plan. Checking yo'self is very black and white. There are no gray areas.

7. Create a Social Media Post

Declare to the world that you are in the crawlin' phase of your life right now. We need to make crawlin' sexy again! Extra points for creativity! There will be a surprise for the winner of the #imcrawlin post.

Use #crawlbeforeyouball #financialmentalhealth #mrsmd and tag @buffiepurselle on IG or FB.

8. Practice Meditation

Practiced for thousands of years, meditation was originally meant to help deepen one's understanding of the sacred and mystical forces of life. These days, meditation is also used for relaxation and stress reduction. It is considered a type of mind-body, complementary medicine that can produce a deep state of relaxation and a tranquil mind. During meditation, focus your attention and eliminate the stream of jumbled thoughts that may be crowding your mind and causing you stress. This process often results in enhanced physical and emotional well-being.

First, find a safe space to sit quietly where you can concentrate on you (uninterrupted) for around 10 minutes. Second, close your eyes and concentrate within on centering yourself. If your mind wanders, that is fine! This practice is about training your mind to come back to concentrating on you. When your mind inevitably starts to drift back to the things you need to do today, simply acknowledge that you need to do those things with kindness, then come back to the meditation. This practice takes time. Remember, we are crawlin', not running! There is a reason that we say the *practice* of meditation because we must practice it. Forgive yourself beforehand to help you get in the right frame of mind. This is a judgment-free zone where you accept what is and don't worry about what is not.

9. Review Wants vs. Needs

This is my favorite step! I bet you think it's easy to determine wants from needs, right? Wrong! Unfortunately, we allow our emotions and that little voice within to coerce us into believing that wants are in fact needs. Please review the definitions as you prepare for your next assignment.

By definition:

A **want** is something you desire
but is not required to have to survive.
A **need** is something you must have in order to live.

Crawl Before You Ball

ASSIGNMENT

. . . .

GRAB YOUR LAST THREE MONTHS of bank statements, credit card statements, and cash receipts. Enter each transaction in the #cb4ub spreadsheet—**https://justbeingbuffie. com/budget**. This spreadsheet requires you to account for each and every expense. You will have to determine whether each purchase is a **NEED** or a **WANT**.

Enter your **REAL** income. Not, if I get a bonus or work overtime-type income, but the income you can count on every month. If you are currently unemployed, please list your unemployment income. If you are a student, list the money that you use to live on each month, including student loans, money from scholarships or your parents, and your job.

Enter your **REAL** liabilities, not your liar-abilities. This is any debt or other financial responsibilities that you owe but are not currently paying. For example, a student loan debt. Remember, I owned a chain of tax practices and was a licensed mortgage broker for years, so I know what folks spend money on each month.

Use the link above to complete your assignment. When you're done, look at your total for monthly wants. This is your new savings.

> ***Play around with this spreadsheet. You can't break it! Have fun with it. See what happens when you cut out some or all of your wants for a few months. This is your TOOL to help you learn how to CONTROL your money instead of allowing your money to CONTROL your life.**

Past students have recalled this assignment as being one of the most revealing and difficult. It can be tedious and grueling to go through each transaction per month. But there is sound reason for why I want you to do this step manually. Doing it on an app is *not* the same. Going through this exercise of seeing how much you spend and earn each month will change your perspective. So . . .

Take your time. It should take you a while to complete.

Please document your journey each day. Jot down how you feel about what's going on in your life. Have you been able to keep to your new budget? How are you handling the inevitable temptations that arise? And how do you feel after meditation? There are thirty pages in this book for you to do just that after the final chapter. Use it as a journal and workbook. Having the ability to come back and see where you were, what your triggers used to be, and how far you've come can help you make meaningful and sustainable, life-lasting change.

CB4UB NEEDS	CB4UB WANTS

BUDGET
PLANNER

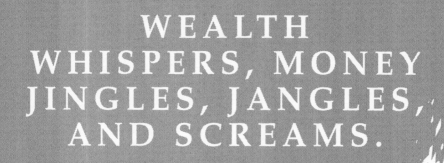

WEALTH
WHISPERS, MONEY
JINGLES, JANGLES,
AND SCREAMS.

MONTH: _____

THIS MONTH'S GOALS

- _____
- _____
- _____
- _____

- _____
- _____
- _____
- _____

INCOME	AMOUNT	SAVINGS	AMOUNT

MON.	TUE.	WED.	THU.	FRI.	SAT.	SUN.

ACTUAL: _____   **PROJECTED:** _____

CASH FLOW SUMMARY

CASH FLOW	CATEGORY	AMOUNT
Total Income		$
Total Expense	All	$
Total Expense	Needs	$
Total Expense	Wants	$
Total Cash Flow	Needs & Wants	$
Total Cash Flow	Needs Only	$

MONTHLY INCOME

MONTHLY INCOME	AMOUNT
Income 1	$
Income 2	$
Extra income	$
Borrowed money	$
Total Income	$

NOTES

....

....

....

....

....

....

MONTHLY EXPENSES

INSURANCE	NEED/WANT	AMOUNT
Home		$
Health		$
Vehicle		$
Life		$
Other		$
		$
Subtotal		$

HOUSING EXPENSE	NEED/WANT	AMOUNT
Mortgage or rent		$
Second mortgage or rent		$
Home phone		$
Mobile phone		$
Electricity		$
Gas		$
Water and sewer		$
Cable / Satellite		$
Internet		$
Security system		$
Waste removal		$
Maintenance or repairs		$
Supplies		$
Other		$
		$
		$
Subtotal		$

TRANSPORTATION	NEED/WANT	AMOUNT
Vehicle 1 payment		$
Vehicle 2 payment		$
Bus / taxi fare		$
Licensing		$
Fuel		$
Maintenance		$
Other		$
		$
		$
Subtotal		$

LOANS	NEED/WANT	AMOUNT
Personal		$
Student		$
School tuition		$
Credit card		$
Credit card		$
Credit card		$
Other		$
		$
		$
Subtotal		$

SAVINGS OR INVESTMENTS	NEED/WANT	AMOUNT
Retirement account		$
Investment account		$
College		$
Other		$
		$
		$
Subtotal		$

PETS	NEED/WANT	AMOUNT
Food		$
Medical		$
Grooming		$
Toys		$
Other		$
		$
		$
Subtotal		$

NOTES

....

....

....

....

....

....

PERSONAL CARE	NEED/WANT	AMOUNT
Medical		$
Hair / nails		$
Clothing		$
Dry cleaning		$
Health club / fitness		$
Organization dues or fees		$
Education		$
Other		$
		$
		$
Subtotal		$

ENTERTAINMENT	NEED/WANT	AMOUNT
Streaming service		$
Subscriptions		$
Movie rental		$
Movies		$
Concerts		$
Sporting events		$
Live theatre		$
Other		$
		$
		$
Subtotal		$

Crawl Before You Ball

TAXES	NEED/WANT	AMOUNT
Federal		$
State		$
Local		$
Other		$
		$
		$
Subtotal		$

FOOD	NEED/WANT	AMOUNT
Groceries		$
Health supplements		$
Dining out		$
Other		$
		$
		$
Subtotal		$

NOTES

....

....

....

....

....

....

....

CHILDREN	NEED/WANT	AMOUNT
Medical		$
Clothing		$
School tuition		$
School supplies		$
Organization dues or fees		$
Organization dues or fees		$
Lunch money		$
Cable / Satellite		$
Childcare		$
Toys / Games		$
Other		$
		$
		$
Subtotal		$

LEGAL	NEED/WANT	AMOUNT
Attorney		$
Alimony		$
Child support		$
Payments on lien or judgment		$
Other		$
		$
		$
Subtotal		$

GIFTS AND DONATIONS (in order of priority)	NEED/WANT	AMOUNT
Birthday gifts		$
Wedding gifts		$
Holiday gifts		$
Charity		$
Other		$
		$
		$
Subtotal		$

SAVINGS BUDGET

SAVING FOR	AMOUNT NEEDED	DUE DATE

MONTHLY BUDGET REVIEW

BALANCE FROM LAST MONTH	AMOUNT
Total income	
Total expenses	
Difference	
Total savings	
BALANCE FORWARD	

MY BIGGEST WINS THIS MONTH

I WILL DO THIS WITHIN ONE MONTH TO IMPROVE

NOTES

Crawl Before You Ball

NOTES

DAY 1

DAY 2

DAY 3

DAY 4

DAY 5

DAY 6

DAY 7

DAY 8

DAY 9

DAY 10

DAY 11

DAY 12

DAY 13

DAY 14

DAY 15

DAY 16

DAY 17

Crawl Before You Ball

DAY 18

DAY 19

DAY 20

DAY 21

DAY 22

DAY 23

DAY 24

DAY 25

Crawl Before You Ball

DAY 26

DAY 27

DAY 28

DAY 29

DAY 30

ACKNOWLEDGMENTS

I HAVE BEEN A PAIN in the arse to the following people whilst writing *Crawl Before You Ball*:

My husband, Dr. David Purselle; my fur babies, Louie and Prada; Linda, a.k.a. Mom; Joe, a.k.a. Dad; my sister, Courtney; nephew sons Jalen, Aiden, and Terrence; Dot Lee, a.k.a. my grammy; Kerry, a.k.a. my mother-in-law; bougie Aunt Carolyn; Uncle Tim; Shawn Brooks; my attorney family, Chuck and June; besties Miriam and Measha; my PR team at Smith; David W.; my other fabulous aunty, Dr. Beverly; Silvia; Monica (AAT); and, last but not least, my very patient editors, Patrice and Paula!

Without your love and support, I would have never been able to begin the revolution that is *Crawl Before You Ball*. I want you to know that I love you all dearly, and I hope that I didn't embarrass you too much. Like my mom always says, "Sharing what you know is far more important than sharing what you have."

Like the latest "it" bag, Buffie Purselle makes personal finance, tax compliance, and small business management fashionable.

BUFFIE PURSELLE IS AN ENTREPRENEUR with over twenty years of expertise in the financial field. As the founder of Buffie, LLC, she derives her success from her professional and innate ability to demystify the daunting world of taxes, personal finance, and small business management with skilled, practical, and sometimes sassy guidance with her clients. She is passionate about teaching financial literacy with her book and e-course, *Crawl Before You Ball*. Buffie is a true Southern belle and is most commonly recognized as a third-generation tax practitioner from a family of tax pros. You may recognize Buffie from season seven of Bravo's "Married to Medicine." She is also recognized as a highly sought-after national tax and personal finance expert seen on HLN, CNN, and CNBC.

Her philanthropic endeavors include being Vice-Chair of IYAI+ (Introducing Youth to American Infrastructure). IYAI+ is a nonprofit founded by Dr. Beverly Scott. Eight years ago, Buffie became severely ill. In the blink of an eye, Buffie's bubbly personality that her friends knew and loved seemed to disappear. She was overcome with chronic fatigue, joint pain, skin rashes, mouth sores, and hair loss. After a year of testing, she was diagnosed with lupus. Buffie is a National Ambassador for the Lupus Foundation of America. She supports initiatives to raise awareness and funds for lupus research. Buffie is happily married to the love of her life, Dr. David Purselle. They have two fur babies, Louie, a toy poodle, and Prada, a Labradoodle.

She lives by the motto,

> *"If you look for the bad in people,*
> *you will surely find it,"*

so she chooses to look for the good.